NATIVE AMERICANS

Projects, Games, and Activities
FOR GRADES K-3

Diane Teitel Rubins

Troll Associates

Metric Conversion Chart
1 inch = 2.54 cm
1 foot = .305 m
1 yard = .914 m
1 mile = 1.61 km
1 square mile = 2.6 square km
1 fluid ounce = 29.573 ml
1 dry ounce = 28.35 g
1 ton = .91 metric ton
1 gallon = 3.79 l
1 pound = 0.45 kg
1 cup = .24 l
1 pint = .473 l
1 teaspoon = 4.93 ml
1 tablespoon = 14.78 ml

Conversion from Fahrenheit to Celsius: subtract 32 and then multiply the remainder by 5/9.

Interior illustrations by Barry Koch

ISBN: 0-8167-3268-X

Printed in the United States of America.
10   9   8   7   6   5   4   3   2   1

TABLE OF CONTENTS

The Sioux

The Tlingit

Supplementary Activities

INTRODUCTION

Native Americans were the first people to live in what is now the United States and Canada. Thousands of years ago, they came from Asia, probably hunting for food. They walked from Siberia to Alaska, most likely, across land that is now covered by water.

When Christopher Columbus landed in the New World in 1492, he thought he had reached India. He called the people he met Indians. Today we call Indians *Native Americans* because they lived in this country long before any European settlers.

When colonists came from Europe to settle North America, they first met Native American tribes on the East Coast. As they moved westward looking for more land, they found Native Americans wherever they went. Sometimes Europeans and Native Americans were friendly and taught each other valuable lessons. But, unfortunately, they often fought over land, and people died.

By 1776 when the United States became a nation, there were about two hundred fifty tribes living in different parts of the country. There was no such thing as *one* Native American way of life. Each tribe lived in different kinds of houses, wore different kinds of clothes, ate different kinds of food, and played different kinds of games. They spoke different languages and practiced different kinds of religions.

The Native American tribes described in this book once included close to a million people in this country. Hundreds of years ago *how* each tribe lived depended a great deal on *where* it lived. So in the same way a New York City child lives differently from a southern Californian child, life for a southeastern Cherokee was quite different from that of a northwestern Tlingit.

In the end, Native Americans lost much of their land to the new settlers and were forced onto reservations. Many Native Americans still live on these separate parcels of land assigned to them by the United States government. Native Americans today struggle to raise their children in a bias-free society.

By studying these Native American tribes, your students will learn about other cultures. A deeper understanding of a people with such a rich and beautiful history can only lead to a greater respect for Native Americans.

Map of Tribal Locations

This map shows the approximate areas where most members of the
ten Native American tribes discussed in this book live today.
Use the map as a reference to complement the
"Information To Share" pages in each chapter.

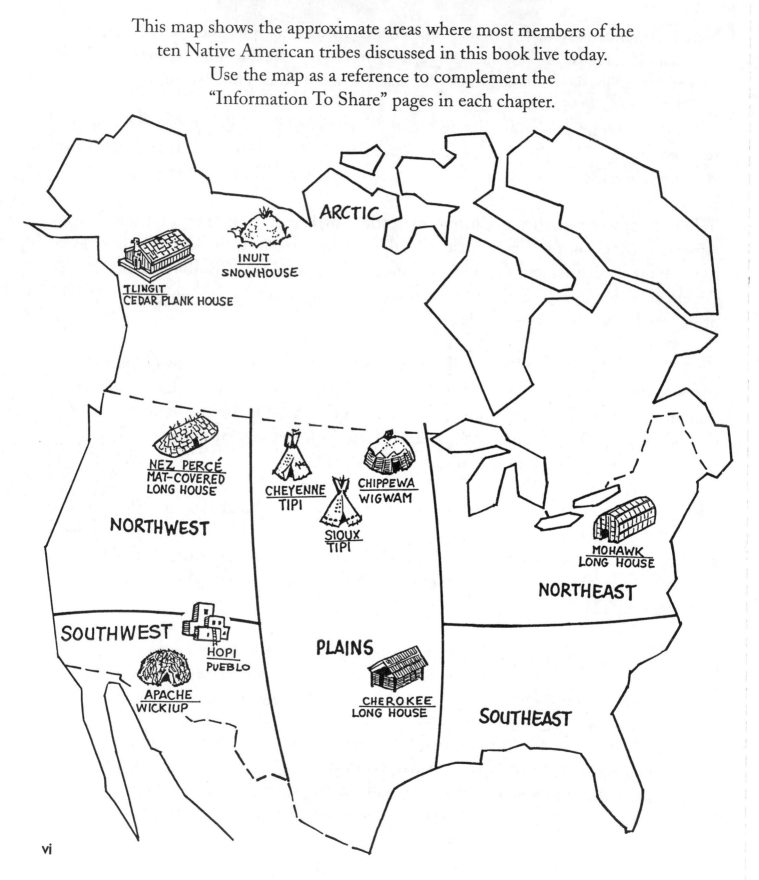

ARCTIC

TLINGIT
CEDAR PLANK HOUSE

INUIT
SNOWHOUSE

NEZ PERCÉ
MAT-COVERED
LONG HOUSE

CHEYENNE
TIPI

SIOUX
TIPI

CHIPPEWA
WIGWAM

NORTHWEST

MOHAWK
LONG HOUSE

NORTHEAST

SOUTHWEST

HOPI
PUEBLO

PLAINS

APACHE
WICKIUP

CHEROKEE
LONG HOUSE

SOUTHEAST

MEET THE
APACHE

WICKIUP

The name Apache came from the Zuñi Indian word *apachu*, meaning "enemy." The Apache called themselves *Tin-ne-ah*, which means "the people." They lived in lands that are now Arizona, New Mexico, Texas, northern Mexico, and parts of Utah, Colorado, and Oklahoma.

Unlike many of their neighbors, the Apache were wanderers. They usually lived in one place for short periods of time and then moved. Adaptable to the plains, desert, or mountains, the five different divisions of the tribe were scattered all over the Southwest.

The women of the tribe built homes called *wickiups*. A wickiup was a small, circular or oval hut framed with thin wooden poles and covered with bundles of grass and tree branches. Smoke from fires built in the earthen floor escaped through a hole in the roof. Apache women also wove beautiful, strong baskets.

BASKETS

Apache men spent most of their time hunting deer, antelope, elk, and, occasionally, buffalo. Before they owned horses, they would hunt on foot, usually alone. Although the lakes and rivers were full of fish, most Apache never caught or ate them.

Apache women and children gathered wild plants, fruits, and vegetables. The yucca and mescal plants were important to their diet. In summer they gathered wild onions, strawberries, raspberries, grapes, and cherries. In the fall they collected acorns and sweet piñon nuts. The Apache seldom farmed, but those who did grew corn, beans, and squash.

Another way the Apache found food was by raiding. To the European settlers it was stealing, but to the Apache it was a necessity. When food was

YUCCA PLANT

scarce, they saw it as the only way to supply themselves with meat. Raiding parties of four to eight men traveled on foot, often a hundred miles or more into enemy territory, grabbed whatever they could carry, and ran. Unfortunately, after the Apache learned to ride horses, the raids became more frequent, more serious, and much more deadly.

Apache women used deer hide to make the family clothing. In warm weather the men and boys wore only breechcloths and the women and girls wore only skirts. In cold weather the men and boys added shirts that hung almost to their knees. The women and girls wore simple dresses with fringe. Everyone wore knee-high deerskin moccasins. After Mexican settlers moved into their territory, the Apache began wearing very colorful cotton clothes but continued to wear moccasins.

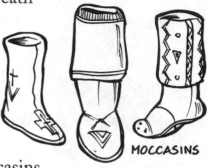
MOCCASINS

In the 1860s the United States Army began its war against the Apache, trying to force them onto reservations. It wasn't until 1886 that the last band, led by a warrior named Geronimo, surrendered. This marked the end of the battle between the United States Army and the Native Americans. Although the government agreed to help those on reservations with money and goods, it took many years to fulfill that promise.

GERONIMO

A DAY IN THE LIFE OF AN
APACHE CHILD

Morning Star, a beautiful Apache girl, lived with her family in a small, grass-covered hut called a *wickiup*. Their camp, with only eight huts, was near water and well-hidden among the piñon trees, where it was safe from enemy attack. The two center wickiups belonged to the camp chief who was the oldest and most skillful hunter. Everyone in the camp was related.

Morning Star's people moved often to new campsites. Usually they moved when the seasons changed or when they had eaten all the wild plants from the nearby hills. Today was moving day. Their new campsite was about one day's travel away. The old *shaman*, or medicine man, predicted that moving there would bring good luck.

After a morning meal of deer meat and vegetables, all the women and their daughters started packing the household goods in bundles. Because their wickiups were so weather-beaten, they would not take them to the new camp. When the huts were empty, the women pulled them apart and dragged the grass and poles away. They felt it was bad luck to leave an old campsite still standing. Once at their new camp, Morning Star and her mother could build a new wickiup in a few hours.

The group walked slowly along the mountain slopes. The women and girls carried the household goods. Some also carried babies in cradleboards on their backs. The men carried only weapons as they kept a watchful eye out for enemies.

In the warm spring sun, the men and boys wore only a breechcloth and the women and girls only skirts. They all wore knee-high moccasins to protect them from thorny plants, rocks, and snakes. And, in spite of the heat, they wore their thick, straight black hair long and loose. They rarely braided it or pulled it back.

As she walked, Morning Star saw signs of spring all around. The hills were covered with pink and white yucca plants in bloom. Other kinds of cactus plants with yellow and red flowers added splashes of color to the journey. In the weeks to come, Morning Star and her mother would use these flowers to make dyes for painting their baskets.

Morning Star looked forward to the fresh food that spring always brought. First she helped her mother harvest the yucca plant. The tender stalks could be roasted or steamed over a large fire in a deep pit filled with stones. Some of the steamed food would be dried, wrapped in animal skins, and stored in baskets until the cold season when food was scarce. Morning Star's favorite chore was making berry cakes. To make these treats, strawberries or raspberries were pounded into cakes and dried in the sun. Then berry juice was poured over the cakes and, as they dried, a sugary coating formed. These fruit cakes lasted a long time without spoiling.

After walking for what seemed like hours, Morning Star was happy that the group was stopping to eat and drink. In the shade of a canyon, everyone sat down to rest. The adults crouched down by the stream and splashed cool water on their faces. Some of the younger children jumped right into the water. Morning Star was content just watching the little ones. She knew that in a short time the march would start again. She would need all her energy to finish the journey to her new home.

Making Apache Shields

The Apache made shields out of animal hides. Each warrior painted on his personal "magic" design. It was often believed that it was the design that kept him safe, not the shield. Here is how students can make their own shields.

What You Need

one large unbreakable bowl,
    about twelve inches in diameter
one large sheet of heavy cardboard
    or oaktag per child
one large piece of solid-colored
    (not patterned) cloth per child

fabric glue
scissors
paint, paintbrushes
elastic, about eight inches per child

What You Do

1. Turn bowl upside-down on each child's piece of cardboard. Have each child trace a large circle around the bottom of the bowl onto their cardboard.

2. Have children cut out their cardboard circles.

3. Tell children to place their cardboard circle on top of a piece of cloth. Have each child draw a circle on the cloth a few inches larger than the cardboard circle.

4. Now have children cut out the cloth circle.

5. Have children place their cardboard circle in the center of the cloth circle. Then carefully spread fabric glue around the edge of the cardboard circle.

6. Next, have them gently pull the edges of the cloth over the cardboard and press them onto the glue. Let the glue dry completely.

7. Now children can paint the cloth side of their shield with their own "magic" design.

8. Have children glue a piece of elastic to the center of the back of the shield so they can carry it on their arm.

11

Name _____ Date _____

A Tiskit, A Tasket, Fill Up Every Basket

Baskets were important to the Apache. Women made strong, colorful baskets from plants, reeds, and herbs that grew wild on the plains, desert, and mountains. They painted the baskets beautiful colors with dyes made from flowers. The baskets were used to carry household supplies, food, and even water.

Fill the baskets below with some foods that the Apache liked to eat like strawberries, onions, corn, beans, or squash. Color the baskets with shades of red, yellow, brown, and light purple, colors that the Apache often used.

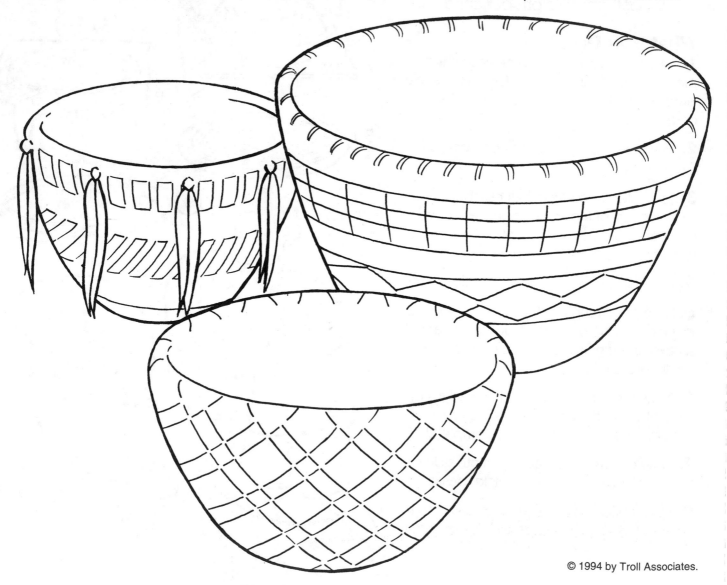

Name_____ Date _____

Good-Luck Charms

The Apache believed that bears, owls, coyotes, snakes, and fish were evil and brought bad luck. They believed crows were a sign of good luck. They also thought of the number four as bringing good luck.

Do you believe in good-luck signs? In each of the four-leaf clovers below, draw a picture of something that you think brings good luck.

Name _____ Date _____

Picture This

Apache women gathered twigs and brush to build a *ramada*, a shady place for cooking, sewing, and childcare. Below is a ramada.

Cut out the pictures below on the dotted lines.
Paste them inside the ramada.
Then color the picture.

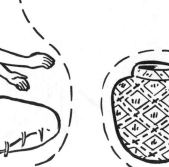

1. Put the woman on the left side.
2. Put the baby in the cradleboard on the right side.
3. Put the basket in front of the woman.
4. Put the dog in the center.

MEET THE
CHEROKEE

Hundreds of years ago, the Cherokee people lived in a beautiful territory of high mountains and thick forests. They lived in the Appalachian and Great Smoky Mountains in parts of what are now the states of Virginia, West Virginia, North and South Carolina, Georgia, Kentucky, Tennessee, and Alabama. At one time the land of the Cherokee covered about forty thousand square miles and included about two hundred towns and villages.

At first these Native Americans lived in caves and rock shelters in the mountains. That is why they became known to neighboring tribes as Cherokee, meaning "cave people." The Cherokee, however, called themselves *Ani'-Yun'wiya,* meaning "real people."

A Cherokee family had two houses—a main house and a smaller house. The family ate and slept in the main house most of the time. This house, in the shape of a rectangle, was made from hickory poles and long, stiff cane plant stems covered with a mixture of clay and grass that dried like plaster. The roof was made from large pieces of chestnut bark. The smaller house, used for sleeping in winter or on cold nights, was low and partly underground. Its cone-shaped roof was made of poles covered with earth. Inside, with only beds and a fire pit, it was smoky but warm.

In spring and summer everyone worked very hard to raise crops of corn, beans, squash, pumpkins, and sunflowers, which were prized for their tasty seeds. The Cherokee grew three kinds of corn, their most

WINTER HOUSE

MAIN HOUSE

GRINDING CORN

important crop. One kind was eaten roasted, another kind was boiled with vegetables, and the third kind was ground into flour to make cornbread.

Cherokee family life was very busy. The men and boys cleared the forest for planting. They hunted large game such as deer and bears with bows and arrows. To hunt birds and smaller animals such as rabbits or opossums, they used a *blowgun*, a weapon made from a hollow reed, through which they shot small darts. Boys were taught to tell time and direction by the position of the sun. Above all, they were taught never to show feelings in front of strangers.

Cherokee girls helped with the women's work, indoors or very close to home. They sewed, gathered firewood, planted and tended crops, cared for babies, cleaned, and cooked. In the evenings they might weave baskets or make pottery. By the time a girl was fourteen, she had all the experience she needed to take care of a home and family of her own.

After 1700 the Cherokee people began having problems with white settlers who wanted their land. They signed many treaties with the Americans, but they were all broken. In 1820 the Cherokee Nation, modeled on the United States government, was formed. But even this organization could not help the Cherokee in the end. In 1838 the Cherokee were forced to move west of the Mississippi River to Indian Territory in what is now Oklahoma. Thousand of people died on this bitter yearlong journey westward. For the Cherokee it was truly, as it came to be known, a "Trail of Tears."

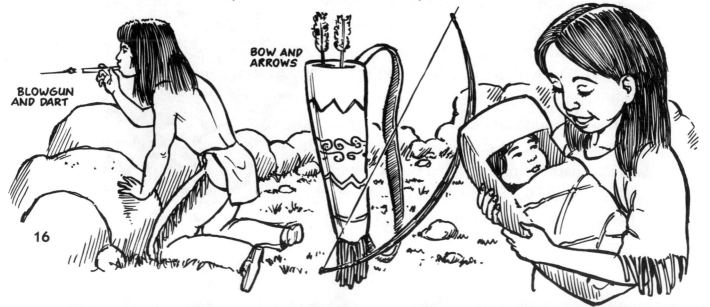

BLOWGUN AND DART

BOW AND ARROWS

A DAY IN THE LIFE OF A
CHEROKEE CHILD

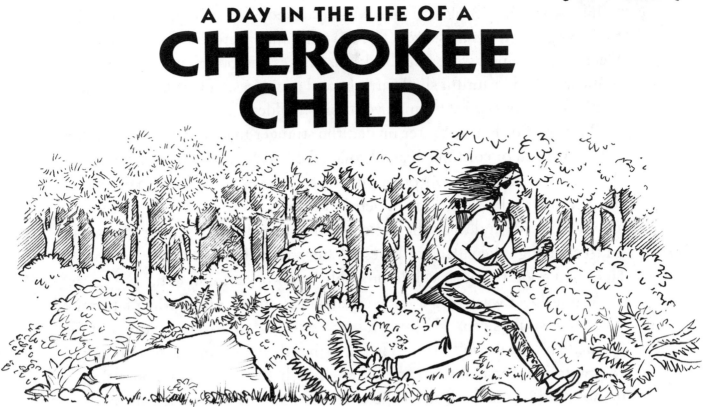

Young Deer, a brave and handsome Cherokee boy about sixteen summers old, was excited to be chosen as his village's messenger. He set off very early to run the fifty miles or so through the rough mountain trails to the Cherokee village of Forest Water. It was very important that he arrive at the village during the day. The Cherokee people knew that friendly visitors always arrived in daylight so they could be welcomed. Only enemies approached after dark.

Young Deer ran swiftly through the hot summer woods, pausing briefly for food and drink. He wore fringed buckskin leggings with a wide buckskin belt, brightly colored moccasins with porcupine quill embroidery, and a heavy necklace of beaver teeth. His hair, long and loose, was tied with an embroidered headband.

When he reached the village of Forest Water, Young Deer headed for the chief's house. It was a little bigger than the other houses. When the chief stepped into view, Young Deer did not speak, since it was up to the older man to speak first. The chief smiled. Without words, Young Deer offered the older man his embroidered tobacco pouch as a gift, a token of friendship.

Young Deer looked with curiosity at the village and its people, so similar to his own. The people of Forest Water looked back at him, interested in the stranger and his message. The boys and men were dressed like Young Deer. The women wore long buckskin dresses and buckskin moccasins. Some also had beautiful shell earrings and necklaces. Their hair was fixed neatly in two braids that hung over their shoulders.

The chief of Forest Water invited the stranger to sit down with him for a delicious meal of corn mush and broiled fish. When they finished eating, the men smoked tobacco from a carved stone pipe. Finally Young Deer decided it was the right time to deliver his message to the chief. Speaking slowly in words and signs, he explained that his village of In the Pines wanted to challenge the village of Forest Water to a ball game. Since both villages had good teams, it would probably be a wonderful match.

Young Deer was given a folded bearskin to spread out on the platform where he would sleep. He hung his bow and case of arrows on the post near the bed and lay down to rest. He knew that the chief would have to talk to the captain of the ball team and other elders before a decision about the game could be made. But for the Cherokee, a good ball game was hard to resist. Young Deer fell asleep knowing that his offer would probably be accepted. He looked forward to leaving at dawn and running home with the good news.

Coiled Clay Pots

The Cherokee made coiled pottery to hold their food and water. Here's how students can make coiled clay pots.

What You Need
one ball of damp clay for each child
one piece of wax paper for each child
small dishes of water
pencils or Popsicle sticks

What You Do
1. Moisten your fingers in the water while working.

2. Knead the ball of clay until it is soft.

3. Pinch off a small piece of clay from the ball. Press this small piece flat on the wax paper until it makes a 3-inch circle about 1/4-inch thick. This will be the base of the pot.

4. Roll the rest of the clay into long coils about as thick as your finger.

5. Start with one clay coil and lay it in a circle on top of the base, as shown. Adding more coils in the same manner, layer upon layer, will build up the pot. Pinch coils together as the pot is built.

6. Turn the pot as you work, moistening the walls with a bit of water and smoothing out any cracks with your fingertips.

7. Finish the pots at about 2-3 inches high. Then make a simple design on each with a pencil point, Popsicle stick, or thumbnail.

8. Let pots dry in the sun. Note: pots are for decorative purposes only, not for eating or drinking.

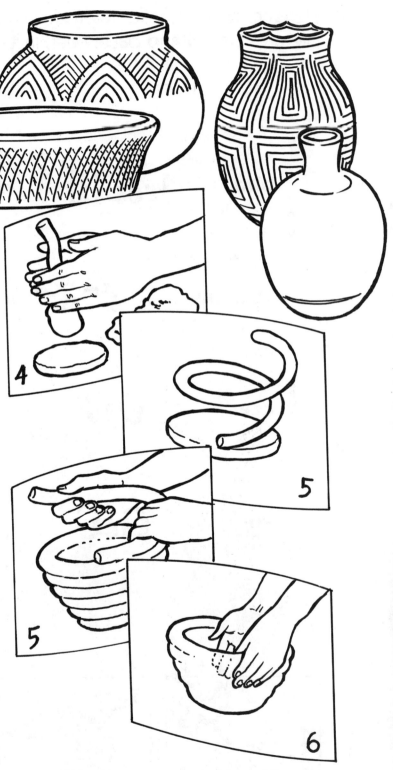

Cherokee Writing

A Cherokee man named Sequoyah invented the Cherokee alphabet.

Here are four Cherokee words. Can you pronounce them? Cut out the pictures below and paste each in its proper box.

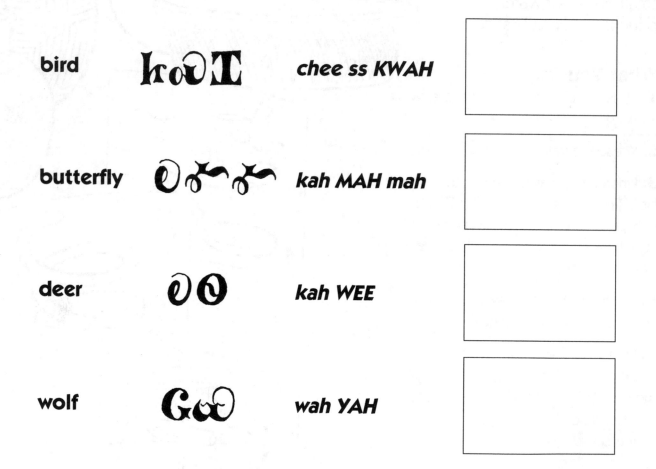

Name_____ Date _____

Colorful Capes

For special occasions Cherokee men and women often wore capes made of turkey feathers. Women sewed the turkey feathers to strips of bark. They then sewed all the strips together.

Color the turkey feather cape.

Name _____ Date _____

Take Me Out
to the Ball Game

The Cherokee played a game with a ball and sticks. The ball was made of deerskin. The sticks had a net on one end. We play a version of this game today. It is called *lacrosse.*

What other sports do you play with a ball? List them below.

_____

_____

_____

_____

_____

MEET THE
CHEYENNE

Very long ago, the Cheyenne people lived in what is now the state of Minnesota. They built villages of earth lodges made of logs, dirt, and grass, and they lived by hunting, fishing, and farming. But their settled way of life changed drastically when they were introduced to horses, which were brought to the Americas by Spanish explorers.

The Cheyenne became expert horseback riders. By hunting on horseback, rather than on foot, they found it easier to kill bison, or buffalo. They gave up farming for hunting and left their permanent villages to live a wandering life, following the buffalo herds that roamed the grassy prairies of the Plains. Buffalo meat made up most of the Cheyenne's food supply. They used the rest of the animal to make clothes, horse gear, coverings for their dwellings, tools, and even fuel.

To suit their new wandering lives, the Cheyenne began living in *tipis* (introduced to them by the Sioux). These cone-shaped houses were made of wood poles covered with as many as twenty buffalo skins sewn together into one large piece. In the center of the tipi was a fireplace, and directly above the fireplace was a smoke hole in the top of the tipi. The outside of a tipi was sometimes painted with stripes, geometric designs, or drawings of buffalo, bear, or other animals. Because tipis could be quickly set up and taken apart, they were

TIPI

perfect for the Cheyenne, who were always moving in search of buffalo herds.

Cheyenne men and women did different types of work. The men fished with willow nets and hunted animals such as buffalo, antelope, wild sheep, deer, and elk with spears and bows and arrows. They also made weapons, served as chiefs, and fought in wars.

Cheyenne women spent most of their time cooking, tanning animal hides, sewing clothes, and making pottery. They gathered berries, nuts, seeds, and lots of turnips, their favorite vegetable. The women did most of the childcare and were also responsible for putting up and taking down the tipis whenever it was time to move.

TANNING A HIDE

Horses played a big part in the lives of Cheyenne children. By age six most of them could ride horses bareback. At that age boys were already helping their fathers train horses. By age twelve boys were going on buffalo hunts and learning about warfare from their fathers and uncles. Girls worked alongside their mothers.

During the middle of the 1800s, the Cheyenne began having trouble with white Americans. The new white settlers were claiming Cheyenne land and killing all the buffalo, the Cheyenne's main source of food. The Cheyenne fought many big battles against United States soldiers, but the United States had a bigger army and better weapons. In the end the Cheyenne were moved onto reservations in Oklahoma and Montana.

A DAY IN THE LIFE OF A
CHEYENNE CHILD

Cold weather was on its way to the Plains, and White Flower's people, the Cheyenne, were busy setting up their winter camp. Building the tipis was the women's work. White Flower watched as her mother and two other women put up a tipi. Though the buffalo hides they used to cover the tipi poles were heavy, the women were able to finish the job in about half an hour.

Because they would stay in this camp for a while, White Flower and her mother would spend more time than usual fixing up the inside of their home. The floor would be covered with raised mats, and benches made of thick matted buffalo robes would provide warmth against the bitter cold to come. A type of cupboard would be fashioned out of buffalo hide. So much of their life depended on the buffalo! White Flower didn't know what her family would do if the buffalo ever disappeared forever and not just for the few winter months.

White Flower helped her mother store the extra clothing that they had brought to their winter camp. She and her mother owned several full-length, sleeveless animal skin dresses that hung below the knee. For winter they would add leggings and buffalo skin robes. For the men and boys, they had made many *breechcloths*—square skins that tied around the waist with a cord. On special occasions the men would wear long-sleeved shirts and fringed leggings. Everyone wore moccasins that were made in two pieces, with hard rawhide soles. And ever since traders had introduced them to colored beads, the women were kept busy sewing rows of beads on almost everything they owned, from belts to moccasins!

After their house was put in order, White Flower went outside with her mother to gather food, not an easy task. They collected fruit from the prickly pear cactus pulling clumps of fruit off the plant. Then they brushed away the spines of the cactus with brooms made of twigs. Protecting their fingers with deerskin thimbles, they carefully picked the fruit clean. Finally they removed the seeds and dried the fruit in the sun. Tonight they would add the pears to the buffalo soup they planned to make.

Like all Cheyenne children, White Flower loved to play and spent a good part of the afternoon doing just that. One of her favorite toys was a little deerskin doll that she took with her everywhere. Her brother's favorite toy was a miniature bow and arrow set. At her age White Flower was still young enough to play with boys. As boys and girls got older, though, they were kept apart, so that the tribe could begin preparing them for their different adult roles.

Today White Flower and other children were playing "camp." They used little tipis made by their mothers and had their dogs drag the materials for

the tipis a short distance from their real homes. When they decided on a good place to set up camp, the children started to pretend. The girls were the mothers, the boys the fathers, their dogs were the horses, and their baby brothers and sisters were their "children." Today at play camp, one of the boys actually caught a fish in a nearby stream, and the girls prepared and cooked it. They all felt so grown-up!

Making a Tipi

The Cheyenne were introduced to the tipi (or tepee) by the Sioux. This portable home was ideal for the wandering Cheyenne. Here's how students can make their own tipis.

What You Need

brown paper (either construction paper
  or paper cut from grocery bags)
crayons, pencils, or markers
glue
toothpicks (three per child)
scissors
one tipi outline for each child

What You Do

1. Distribute one tipi pattern to each child.

2. Have children trace the tipi outline onto the brown paper with a pencil. They must press hard to make the outline show up.

3. Have children use crayons or markers to make colorful designs on their tipis.

4. Cut out each tipi. Fold at dotted line and spread a thin layer of glue from top to bottom of TAB.

5. Make a cone shape with the paper, and glue TAB to other outside edge. Let the glue dry.

6. Cut a small slit on the seam for an entrance flap.

7. Insert a few toothpicks in the tiny hole at the top. If necessary, use glue to keep them in place.

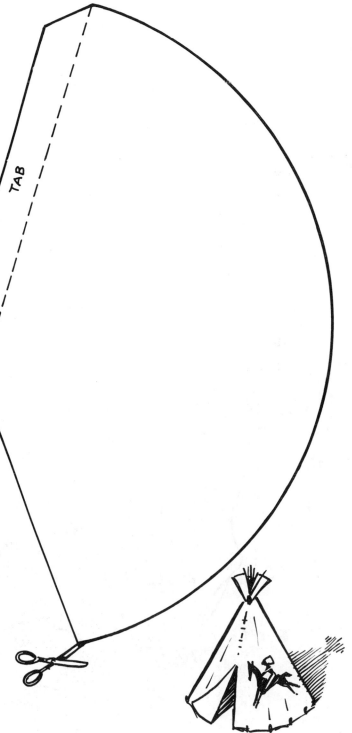

Name _____ Date _____

Hide-and-Seek

Connect the dots to find out what animal weighed about two thousand pounds, was six feet high, and could outrun a horse.

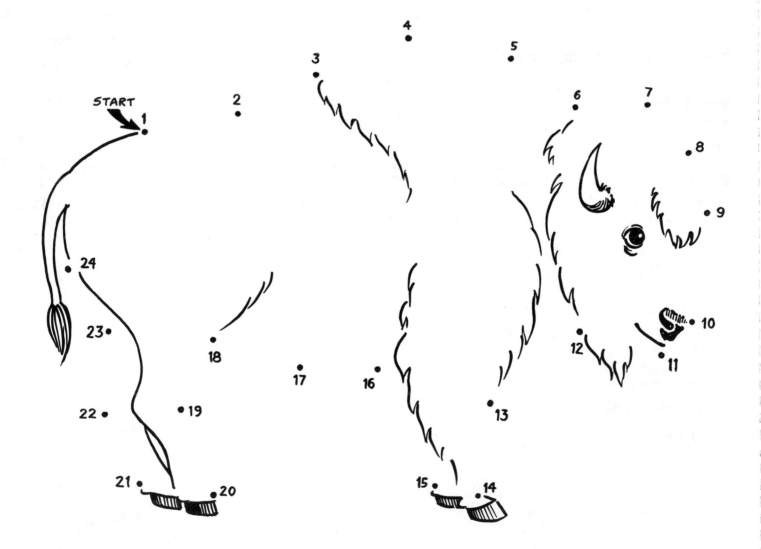

Name_____ Date _____

Designing a Cheyenne Village

Use colored pencils, crayons, or markers to draw a Cheyenne village on this page. Draw three tipis. Draw two horses. Draw two children playing with a dog. If you like, add other people, animals, or plants.

Cheyenne

Name _____ Date _____

Picture Stories

Many Native Americans used picture writing to tell a story without using words. The Cheyenne drew picture stories on animal skins.

Draw a picture story on the "skin" below. Use your own pictures to tell the story.

MEET THE
CHIPPEWA

The Chippewa, also called the Ojibwa, were people of the Northern Woodlands. About two hundred years ago they were living along the shores of Lake Superior, Lake Michigan, and Lake Huron in what are now the states of Michigan, Wisconsin, and Minnesota. They spread as far west as North Dakota and as far north as Ontario, Canada.

GATHERING RICE

Although the Chippewa grew some of their food in gardens, they also traveled at different times of year to hunt and gather food. In small, permanent settlements near river or lake shores, the Chippewa women spent the summers caring for gardens and picking wild berries, while the men and boys fished and trapped. In the fall they moved to their rice fields to gather wild rice, their basic year-round food. In winter they lived in the forests, away from the bitterly cold winds that blew across the rivers and lakes. In early spring they traveled to the maple groves to make maple sugar.

WIGWAM

Most Chippewa families slept in a dome-shaped hut called a *wigwam*. A wigwam was a simple framework of about twenty poles arranged in a circle and pushed firmly into the ground. The poles were bent at the top and tied with roots or with tough animal tendons called *sinew*. The men were responsible for building the frame. The women then had the job of covering the frame with sheets of elm or birch bark or with mats woven from plants called bulrushes. In cold weather they used both a layer of bark over a layer of mats. A moose hide was hung in the doorway. Inside the wigwam cedar

SNOWSHOES

MOCCASINS

branches and rush mats covered the ground. Beds were made out of spruce boughs covered with animal skins. Rolled up animal skins and hides were used as seats.

In addition to helping build and repair the wigwams, Chippewa women and older girls were also responsible for the long, hard task of making clothes and moccasins from animal skins. They also made jewelry from shells, bones, or animal claws. Other female chores included cooking, weaving, embroidering, picking nuts and berries, gathering wild rice, and boiling sap into maple sugar.

The Chippewa men and older boys spent most of their time hunting, trapping, and fishing for food. Excellent hunters, they knew the habits of animals and were good at catching them with bows and arrows, stone axes, or baited traps. They brought home large animals such as moose, elk, deer, and bear, as well as smaller game such as beaver, porcupine, rabbit, and mink. Hooks, spears, and nets were used to catch fish.

Younger Chippewa children usually stayed close to the wigwams and played with tops, dolls, marbles, toy canoes, and toy toboggans. Sometimes they danced animal or war dances like those the adults did. Both boys and girls competed in snowshoe and toboggan races and enjoyed playing blindman's buff. They also loved listening to the stories and legends that the old men would tell in the evenings.

The Chippewa traveled a lot during the year and relied on different means of transportation. Trees provided the materials for their most useful inventions: the canoe, the snowshoe, and the toboggan. Each family owned several birch-bark canoes, all of them in constant use during the spring, summer, and fall. Snowshoes, made from the branches of ash trees and moose-hide strips, were a necessity in deep winter snows. And lightweight toboggans, in addition to providing a fun winter pastime, made it easier to carry heavy loads over narrow forest trails.

A DAY IN THE LIFE OF A
CHIPPEWA CHILD

One bright, crisp September morning, Big Brother was busily loading three canoes. These were the boats his family would paddle from their summer home to their rice fields. The canoes would carry bundles of food, sleeping mats, blankets, cooking pots, extra clothes, and moccasins. Big Brother, Big Sister, and their dog would travel in the first canoe. Grandmother and Little Brother would take the second canoe. And Father, Mother, and Little Sister would paddle the third.

Big Brother's family had an old shelter near the rice fields. When they arrived, they patched it up with a few mats and put their belongings inside. After praying to the Great Spirit, the Master of Life, and thanking him for the rice crop, the family got into their canoes to start gathering the rice. They paddled their light, round-bottomed canoes along the shallow shores of the lake, where wild rice grows best. Big Brother paddled one canoe, and his mother sat at the other end of the boat, facing him. Her job was to reach out and hook the plants with a stick, then shake the grains into the bottom of their canoe.

When the canoes were filled with grain, the family returned to shore and emptied the rice onto large mats so it could dry in the sun. After it dried, the rice was cleaned and cooked. For morning meals rice was usually boiled in water without any added flavoring. For evening meals it was usually sweetened with maple sugar. Tonight's meal made Big Brother especially proud—and full. Earlier in the day he and his brother had shot several wild ducks. Big Sister had cleaned them and roasted them on tall sticks over coals in the fire pit. Eating wild rice with duck was a special treat, and Father had invited a few neighbors to share in their feast.

Big Brother enjoyed rice-gathering time, but he knew that soon snow would come and the family would be returning to their winter wigwam. With enough food stored for the long, cold weather, he was sure that his family would be well-fed, safe, and warm. During the winter nights he would sleep soundly under his thick rabbit-fur blankets, dreaming about maple-sugar time—a sure sign of spring.

A Taste of Wild Rice

Wild rice, the most important food of the Chippewa people, is still enjoyed today. Also known as Indian rice or water oats, wild rice is actually the seed of a grass that grows wild along the edges of lakes in Minnesota, Wisconsin, and southern Canada. Its taste and texture are distinctively different from those of white rice.

Help your students to take a taste trip back in time. Though the Chippewa boiled the rice with no seasoning except for maple sugar, you might want to try this updated version of their old standby.

What You Need
1 cup wild rice
4 cups boiling water
1 teaspoon salt
4 tablespoons butter or
    margarine

What You Do
1. Rinse the dry rice several times in cold water, pouring off any foreign particles. Drain it.

2. Stir it slowly into 4 cups boiling water with 1 teaspoon salt. Simmer about 40-50 minutes, or until the grains are tender and have absorbed all the water.

3. If desired, stir in the butter or margarine, toss with a fork, and serve. Makes about 3 cups of rice.

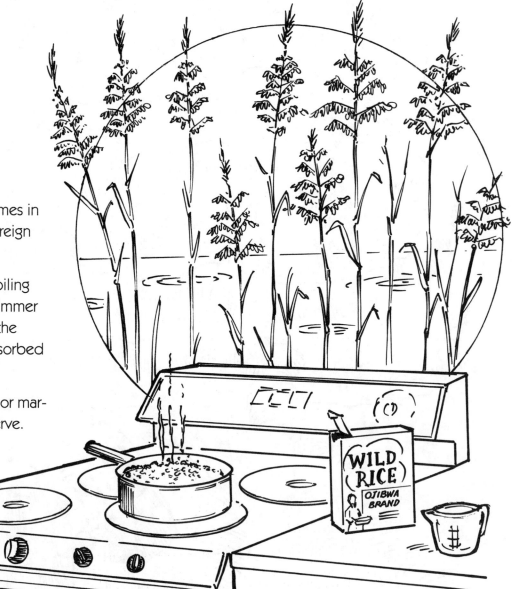

Name _____ Date _____

Can You Canoe?

Help the Chippewa children paddle their canoe to the wigwam. Draw a line with a pencil from start to finish. Do not cross any lines.

Name_____ Date _____

Feet First

The Chippewa people wore beautiful moccasins.

Decorate the pair of Chippewa moccasins on this page. Use the designs on this page for ideas.

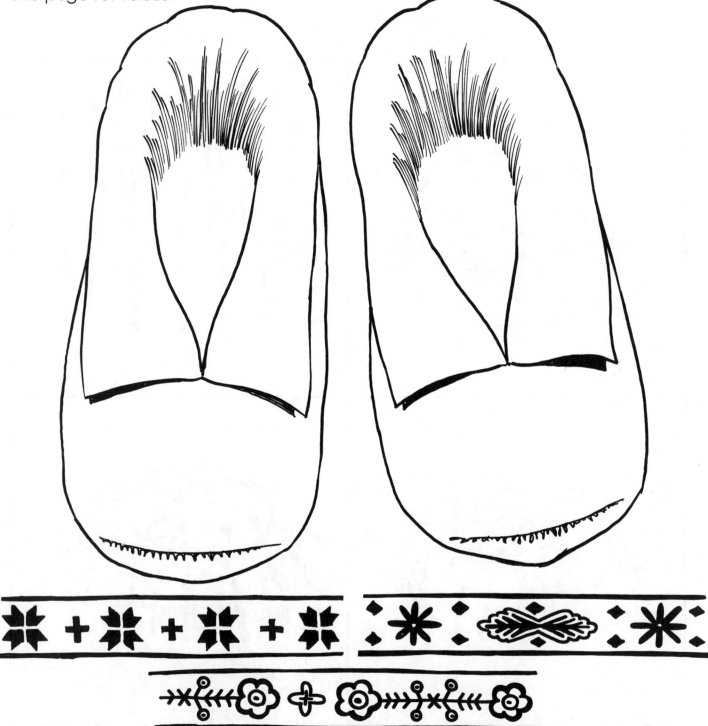

Building a Wigwam

The pictures below show how to build a wigwam. Cut the pictures apart, put them in order, and staple them together. You'll have a little book showing how a wigwam is made.

MEET THE HOPI

In the southwestern desert of what is now the state of Arizona lies the land of the Hopi. Several hundred years ago, before there was a nation called the United States, this hot, dry region was home to thousands of people.

The Hopi villages, or *pueblos* (the Spanish word for *villages*), were built high above the desert floor on large, flat-topped, steep hills called *mesas*. Hopi houses were made of stone covered with wet clay or mud.

Some homes were three or four stories high, and the Hopi used ladders to reach the upper floors. The houses, all joined together, looked like a large, spread-out apartment building.

Throughout history, the Hopi chose to be farmers rather than warriors. They did not need chiefs to rule them or lead them to war. The Hopi were ruled by their religious beliefs and by the Hopi Way—to be kind to everyone and everything.

Hopi men, women, and children all had their own special jobs. The women owned the houses and land. They built the homes, cooked, wove baskets, and made pottery. The men hunted, planted and harvested crops, wove cloth for the family's clothes, and performed most of the religious ceremonies.

MAN WEAVING CLOTH

WOMAN WEAVING BASKET

Hopi children worked with their parents from the time they were about eight years old. The boys learned farming and would go with their fathers to tend the crops. The girls helped their mothers build the walls of their pueblo homes with moist clay dug out of the desert. They also used this clay to make pottery. Girls also helped with the important task of grinding dried corn into flour. After mixing this corn flour with

PLASTERING WALLS

water, they baked paper-thin pieces of bread called *piki*.

Hopi men and boys were well known for their abilities to run fast and to travel far on foot. They needed these abilities because the Hopi had to plant their crops near water sources. The nearest water sources were often far below their mesa-top villages and sometimes more than ten miles from home! Daily climbing and running to look after their crops made the Hopi exceptional long-distance runners.

Music was a big part of Hopi life. The people loved to sing and had a song for almost every daily chore. Whether they were planting, harvesting, or grinding corn, the Hopi would sing about their tasks. Even the way they talked was musical. Hopi legend says that their musical speech was taught to them by the mockingbird.

CORN

PUEBLO VILLAGE

TURQUOISE AND SILVER JEWELRY

SQUASH BLOSSOM HAIRSTYLE

KACHINA DOLL

A DAY IN THE LIFE OF A
HOPI CHILD

Mist-in-the-Morning awoke to a bright, hot, dry desert day. She lived in a Hopi village built high above the desert on a flat-topped, steep hill called a *mesa*. She folded her soft, rabbit-skin blanket and hung it neatly on a pine pole. After a quick breakfast of cooked cornmeal, she was ready to start her day.

It was going to be a hot day, but Mist-in-the-Morning felt cool and comfortable in her family's pueblo. Her father had built the foundation for the house, but she, her mother, and grandmother had built the rest of the house. They used stones covered with mud to make walls that dried smooth and strong in the sun. Because Hopi homes were built with no windows or doors on the ground floor, everyone had to climb in and out of the house on a ladder! All the homes were built around an open plaza, where everyone in the village met for religious ceremonies and dances.

Like all young, unmarried Hopi girls, Mist-in-the-Morning wore her hair in buns on either side of her head. They were meant to look like the blossoms of the squash plant. Once married, the women wore their hair in two long braids. Most girls wore a simple cotton dress colored blue with dye from sunflower seeds. On their feet they wore moccasins made of animal skins.

Mist-in-the-Morning's first chore of the day was to go with her mother to the river below for water. As she came out of their doorway, Mist-in-the-Morning tried placing the large water pot on top of her head. It was quite wobbly at first, but she was getting better at it every day. Walking very straight, she climbed down the mesa toward the river. Today she would try not to spill even one drop on her return trip!

Yesterday Mist-in-the-Morning had begun weaving a basket all by herself. She was making it out of dried, twisted plant leaves. The desert provided many plants for the Hopi to use. Some were cooked and eaten, and some were used for fuel. Other plants were picked to make brushes and paints and dyes for coloring their pots, baskets, and clothes. All Hopi girls learned about plants and their many uses at an early age.

Today Mist-in-the-Morning will help her mother and grandmother make pottery. It is one of her favorite chores! They will make cooking pots, bowls, and jars for water. The part she likes best is decorating the finished pieces. Using a brush made from yucca leaves, she will carefully paint her work with earth colors such as brown, red, orange, yellow, and black.

In the early evening, before the men return from working in the fields, Mist-in-the-Morning will help her mother cook. Once in a while her family eats meat, but not too often because there are not many animals in the desert for the men to kill. So most of the time, a Hopi family eats something made with corn. Tonight they will make a thin cornbread called *piki*. Piki bread can be red, yellow, blue, or white, depending on the color of the corn used to make it. Tonight, they will grind blue corn flour. When it's ready, the wafer-thin bread will be crisp, crunchy, and sweet. As they work, she and her mother will sing a corn-grinding song that will make their job more fun.

Like all Hopi children Mist-in-the-Morning looks forward to the special ceremony to remind the spirits that rain is needed. Her people believe that it is the *kachinas*, or great spirits, who send rain. Since most of their food comes from the land, rain is very important. Soon the whole village will watch as Hopi men, dressed up as kachinas, lead the prayers. After the ceremony Mist-in-the-Morning and her friends will be given tiny kachina dolls, not to play with, but to study.

Kachina Masks

The Hopi believed in magical beings they called *kachinas*, powerful spirits that helped and protected them. There were hundreds of kachinas—each with a different face, clothes, and ornaments. At special times Hopi men dressed up as kachinas by putting on kachina masks. Here's how children can make their own kachina masks.

What You Need

one large, brown paper bag for each child

brightly colored markers and/or paints and paintbrushes

cardboard cylinders (from empty paper towel rolls, plastic wrap, foil, etc.) or paper cups

construction paper

feathers and yarn

glue

scissors

What You Do

1. Show the children how to cut out two holes in the paper bag for eyes. (This works best if they first put the bags over their heads and use a crayon to mark where the eyeholes should be.)

2. Provide markers and/or paints and paintbrushes for children to draw teeth, hair, ornaments, and a face design on the bag. Use the pictures on this page for ideas.

3. Students can add construction paper, or yarn fringe, cardboard, paper-cup horns, and real or paper feathers.

4. Take pictures of the children in their kachina masks.

Name _____ Date _____

Colorful Corn

To most of us, corn is either yellow or white. But the Hopi grew corn in all colors—yellow, white, black, blue, pink, and even speckled!

Color the ears of corn in the different colors that the Hopi grew.

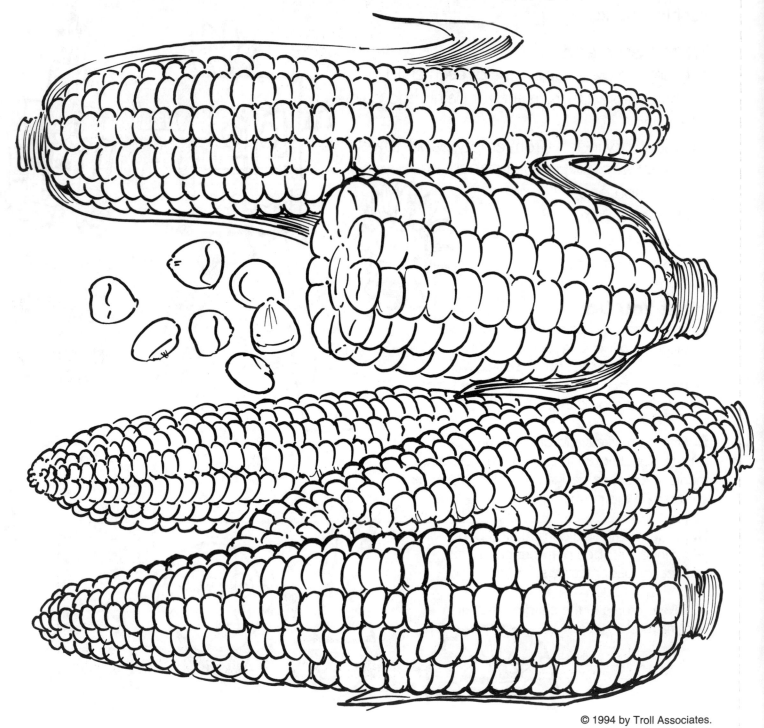

Pueblo Puzzle

Cut out these jigsaw pieces and put them together to make a complete pueblo village. Paste your completed puzzle on a piece of cardboard and color the picture.

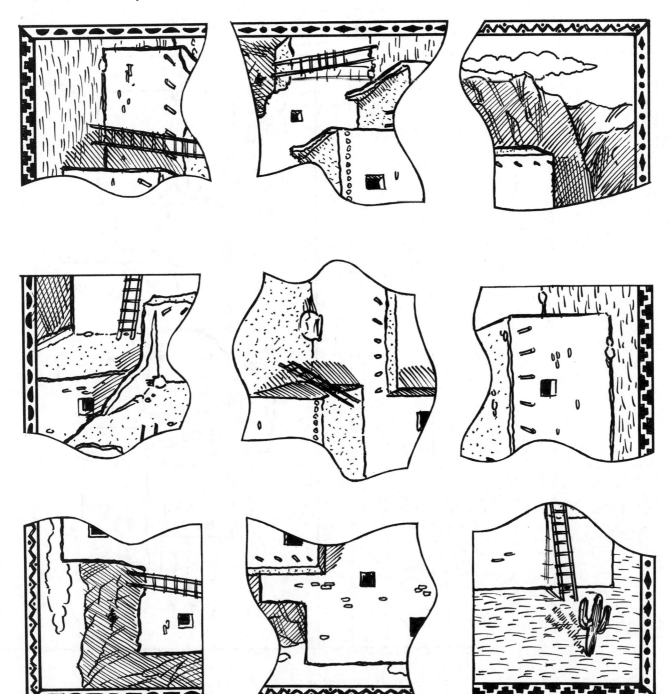

Wish You Were Here

Pretend that you visited a Hopi village. On the postcard below write to a friend about your visit. Write your friend's name and address on the card. Design a stamp for your card.

Now color the picture side of the postcard. Then cut out the two sides and glue them back to back.

MEET THE
INUIT

Near the top of the world, in a treeless, snow-covered land that is now called Alaska and Canada, lived the Inuit. In the harsh, frozen life of the far North, the Inuit diet included raw foods. That's why the Algonquin called the Inuit *Eskimo*, which means "eater of raw meat." Inuit, the name the Eskimo prefer, means "the people."

The Inuit had long, dark, very cold winters and short, cool summers. From September to June, snow covered the ground, and ice covered the ocean, lakes, and streams. Only the top few inches of ground would thaw out completely during the short summer season.

Because farming was impossible, the Inuit lived by the sea and survived by hunting and fishing. They hunted with bows and arrows, as well as spears. Seals, walruses, caribou, polar bears, whales, and fish provided food, fuel, and materials to make boats, tents, tools, weapons, and clothing.

HUNTING POLAR BEAR

DOG SLED

The Inuit moved a lot in their never-ending search for food. Hunters sometimes traveled on foot, but mostly used sleds pulled by powerful dogs called *huskies*. In warmer weather they traveled on water, using boats made of animal skins stretched over bone or wood frames. The quiet and speedy *kayak* was a boat built for one person, who slid into it through a tight-fitting hole at the top. The *umiak* was a larger open boat used to carry about 10 to 12 people and their supplies.

UMIAK

KAYAK

The Inuit traveled in small groups of several families, totaling about forty to one hundred people. Men were the home builders.

Sod houses, the most permanent dwellings, had frames of driftwood and whalebone with sod piled on the roof and against the sides for insulation. In winter camps the Inuit built snowhouses from blocks of thick, hard-packed snow. Light came through a block of clear ice fit into the ceiling or wall. A tunnel entrance

SNOWHOUSE

kept the wind out and the heat in. In spring when the snowhouses started to melt, the Inuit moved into tents, made with wooden poles and covered with caribou skins.

Men were hunters and made the family's boats, sleds, tools, snowshoes, and weapons. Men also took care of the sled dogs and decided where and when the family would travel. Women took care of the house, cooked, prepared the animal skins, and made and mended clothes.

Women did most of the child-rearing, nursing their children and carrying them on their backs until they were almost three years old. Young children led a carefree life of playing, sleeping, and eating whenever they wanted. But by the age of nine or ten, they had to start learning the skills they would need as adults.

The Inuit lived a dangerous and difficult life, but they truly believed that their homeland was the best of all possible worlds. These people, who struggled every day just to keep warm, called their Arctic surroundings "The Beautiful Land."

A DAY IN THE LIFE OF AN
INUIT CHILD

Winter was the most difficult season for Aknik and his family. The below-freezing temperatures turned his Arctic homeland into a wilderness of snow and ice. Daylight lasted for only a few hours. People even farther north had only darkness because the sun never rose—from October to February there was one long night. Because of the darkness, and because many Arctic animals went south for the winter or were sleeping under the ice, hunters had a hard time finding food for their families.

Aknik's family was spending the winter living in a camp near the sea, where they could hunt seals and other animals that they desperately needed. No matter how much food a family managed to store up beforehand, they always needed more to get through these cold, cruel months.

It had taken Aknik and his father a few hours to build a large, dome-shaped snowhouse for their family. His father had cut blocks of snow with a long ivory knife. Then they stacked the blocks in circular rows. To make a skylight, they fit a block of clear ice into the ceiling. Inside, they sculpted eating and sleeping platforms out of snow and covered them with twigs and furs. Using soft rocks called *soapstone*, Aknik carved oil lamps that provided heat and light using *seal blubber*, the thick layer of fat just under the animal's skin. The lamp was also used as a stove. Mother hung a pot over the flame and melted the ice and snow for drinking water.

In the winter, hunting was risky and unpredictable. So Aknik and his family always shared food with others in their group. He and his father might be lucky one day, then catch nothing for weeks after that. Sharing meant that as long as someone in the group could find food, no one would go hungry. Today, Aknik and his father would try their luck at hunting seal. He prayed that, with the help of their huskies, they would be successful.

Aknik went inside to say good-by and to get dry clothes. Good cold-weather clothing was important in the Arctic because freezing to death was a very real threat. Aknik's best clothes were made of warm, lightweight caribou skin. A typical outfit for men, women, and children included a coat with a hood, pants, stockings, mittens, and shoes or boots. Because of the extreme cold, today Aknik dressed in two of each of the garments. He wore the inner layer with the fur against his skin, and the outer layer with the fur facing out. His sealskin boots were waterproof, and his fur mittens had two thumbs. If one side got wet, he could turn the mitten around to the dry side without taking the glove off his hand.

Outside, the family's dog sled was ready. Aknik poured water over the sled's wood runners and watched it instantly freeze. Now they would glide more easily over the trail of rough ice. The five huskies hitched to the sled greeted Aknik with friendly barks. He spoke to them soothingly and checked that the small sealskin booties to protect their feet from ice splinters were secure. Although the dogs were so strong they each could pull a hundred or more pounds, people rarely rode on the sled. Instead they walked or trotted alongside, using the sled to carry their heavy load of supplies.

Aknik learned from his father that in winter one needed good sled dogs and lots of patience to be a successful hunter. The dogs were good at sniffing out the seals' breathing holes that were not visible to men staring at a sea of ice. Once these were found, he watched as his father put a thin, ivory rod through the crust of the snow covering the breathing holes. Then they settled down to wait for the rod to jiggle, signaling them that a seal was near the hole.

Aknik and his father carved seats out of snow and sat down with pieces of fur under their feet to keep them warm and comfortable while they waited. Aknik needed to be patient because it might be hours before they could harpoon a seal. Finally after five long hours, the rod moved, and the men acted quickly. Aknik was grateful that his family and friends would not go hungry tonight.

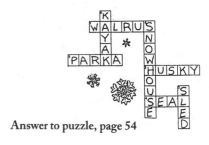

Answer to puzzle, page 54

50

Good-Luck Necklaces

The Inuit wore a tooth necklace for decoration and for good luck. It was supposed to give an Inuit hunter strength and power over seals, whales, and walruses. Here's how students can make a seal-tooth necklace.

What You Need

self-hardening clay

string, cord, or ribbon (two feet per child)

nail for teacher (one for each child optional)

What You Do

1. Have the children make tooth shapes out of the clay. The shapes should be irregular and uneven. (Draw sample shapes on the blackboard.) Each necklace will need about forty "teeth," about one-half-inch wide.

2. Before the clay hardens, use a nail to make a hole for stringing the teeth. Be sure that the holes are large enough to allow the string to fit through them. (If children are old enough, they can use nails to make the holes.)

3. Let clay teeth harden.

4. String the teeth onto the string, cord, or ribbon. Tie the loose ends together.

Inuit
Animal Memory Game

Two people can play this game. Cut out the boxes. Mix up the pictures and lay them face down. Turn over two cards. If they match, keep them. If they do not, put them back in the same places. The next player does the same thing. The player with the most cards wins.

Name_____ Date _____

Winter Wonderland

The Inuit winter was very long, dark, and cold. What is winter like where you live? Pretend you are looking out your window on a winter day. Draw what you see.

Name _____ Date _____

Crossword Puzzle

Look at the picture clues below. Find a word in the Word Box that matches each picture. Write the words in the blank puzzle.

Picture Clues

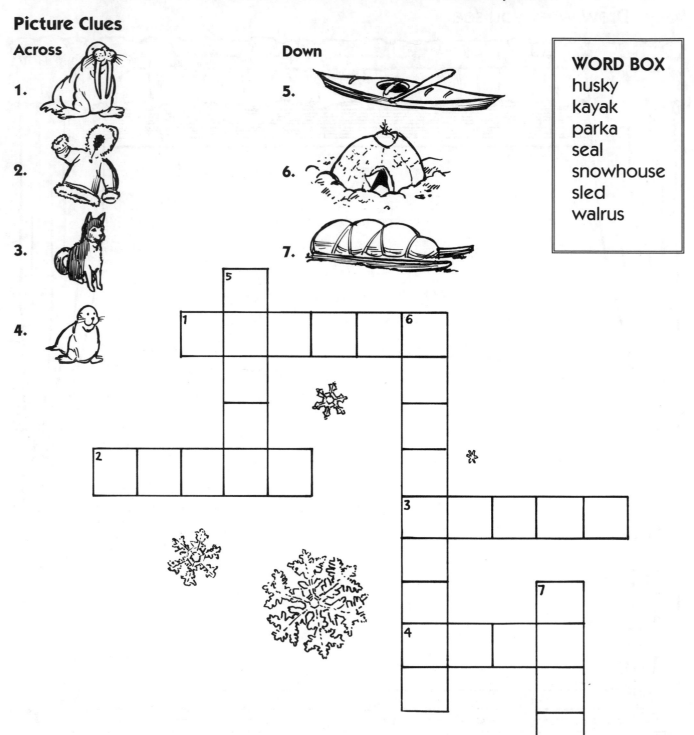

Across

1.

2.

3.

4.

Down

5.

6.

7.

WORD BOX
husky
kayak
parka
seal
snowhouse
sled
walrus

MEET THE MOHAWK

More than five hundred years ago, long before explorers came to America, the Mohawk lived in the beautiful, rich lands of what is now north central New York State. They called themselves *Kanye keha-ka*, or "people of the place of flint." Their enemies called them *Mohawk*, meaning "eater of men."

LONG HOUSE

Mohawk long houses were like narrow barns made of elm poles covered with thick sheets of elm bark. As many as ten families, or about fifty people, lived in each long house. A row of fires was built down the middle for the many families who lived in separate rooms on either side.

Each village had a dozen or so long houses. Surrounding the village was a high wall of sharp, pointed logs called a *palisade*. The single entrance to the village was closely guarded.

The Mohawk's main foods, which they called "the three sisters," were corn, beans, and squash. They enjoyed mushrooms, berries, and nuts, as well as sunflowers and leafy plants. Fish was plentiful, and deer, bear, wild fowl, and small animals supplied them with meat.

SQUASH
CORN
BEANS

Most Mohawk clothing was made from deerskin. The men and boys wore embroidered leggings, seamed in front, without fringe. They also wore breechcloths and, in colder weather, fringed shirts. On special occasions, they wore a short skirt. Warriors shaved their heads to a thin strip and attached a deer tail which stood up straight like bushy hair. Then they added one or two eagle feathers for decoration.

The women and their daughters wore their long hair in braids. They dressed in deerskin skirts and leggings. In winter they added a cape-like blouse with fringe. Everyone owned beaver fur robes, caps, and mittens for cold weather. Moccasins were made of leather or of corn husks.

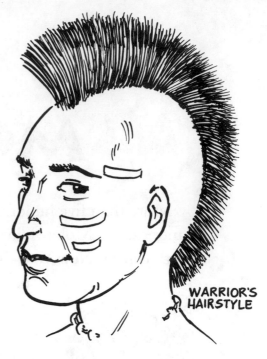

WARRIOR'S HAIRSTYLE

Mohawk women took care of the long house, farmed, raised the children, and made many important tribal decisions. The men cleared the fields, hunted, fished, and went to war. Small boys and girls helped their mothers. At age eight the boys began to learn hunting and fighting. When a girl reached the age of ten, she worked by her mother's side all day.

The Mohawk often fought with four neighboring tribes who spoke the same basic language. Prior to 1400, the Mohawk, Oneida, Onondaga, Cayuga, and Seneca tribes agreed to stop fighting. They formed a strong, peaceful group—the first democracy in America. They called themselves *Haudenosaunee* or "people of the long house," because their lands were next to each other, like families living under one long house roof. Their Algonquin enemies called them "poisonous snakes," a word which sounded like *Iroquois* to the French settlers.

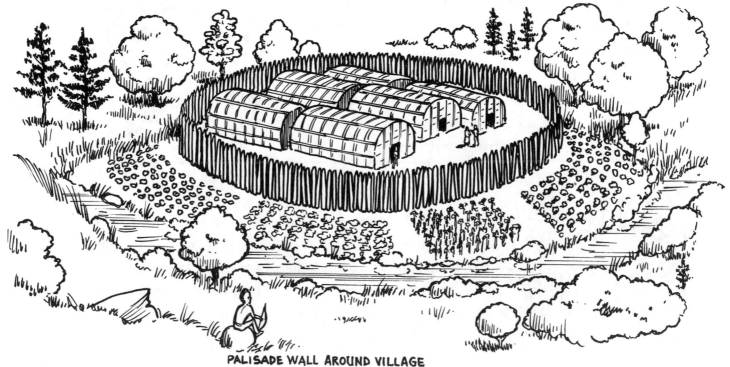

PALISADE WALL AROUND VILLAGE

A DAY IN THE LIFE OF A
MOHAWK CHILD

Beautiful Dawn, nine summers old, lived with her parents, brother, and nine other families in a long house. Her Mohawk village had more than a dozen long houses surrounded by a fence of high, pointed posts. The inside of her house was one huge, long room divided by bark walls. Each family had their own small area for sleeping and storing their belongings. Although the long house had no windows, there were doorways at each end covered with bearskins. Animal skins and woven mats covered the dirt floor. Dried food hung on indoor poles.

Beautiful Dawn's family shared a fire with the family across from them. In cold weather, with the fires always burning, the house got very smoky. Beautiful Dawn knew that by next summer the whole village would have to move. Mohawk villages lasted about ten years. After that, the farmlands around the village were no longer fertile, and the long houses became worn and leaky.

Beautiful Dawn and her family spent most of their time in and around their village. But in late fall and early winter, the Mohawk men hunted many weeks for animals to supply the village with meat during the long winter. Deer hunting was especially important to Beautiful Dawn's people. If animals were not plentiful in the nearby forests, then everyone would leave the village for several months to look for new hunting grounds.

Today the autumn air was crisp and inviting. Beautiful Dawn and her little brother went with their mother early in the morning to their patch of farmland outside the village. While her brother scared away crows, Beautiful Dawn helped her mother tend the crops. The farmland (like the long houses) belonged to the women. They had much to do before the long, harsh winter.

Back from the fields, Beautiful Dawn and her mother prepared the family meal. The Mohawk usually ate only one meal a day, in the late morning.

Today they made *succotash*, one of Beautiful Dawn's favorite foods, by boiling corn and beans together.

They kept the leftover food in a pot hanging over the fire all day long so that people could help themselves whenever they got hungry.

After the meal Beautiful Dawn helped her mother husk corn. Corn provided the Mohawk with so much besides food! They wove the husks into hammocks, mats, baskets, and slippers. From crushed green cornstalks they made a lotion to put on cuts, which they covered with a clean, dry corn-husk bandage. Dried cornhusks were used as fire kindling, and corncobs were used for brushes, back scratchers, and pipes. Corn kernels were strung and worn as necklaces by both men and women. Beautiful Dawn was quite good at making corn-husk dolls—but without faces. The Mohawk believed that if a doll had a face, it might come to life.

CORNHUSK DOLL

As the evening grew cold, everyone returned to the long houses. Safely inside, Beautiful Dawn finished weaving a basket and watched her father carve cups and bowls out of wood. But when the old men started their storytelling, everyone in the long house paid close attention. It was a Mohawk custom that stories were told only inside the long house on cold nights. And no one could fall asleep during a story!

One of the family's favorite stories was about Dekanawidah and how he united the Iroquois people. According to the legend, he saw five tribes sitting together under the branches of a great tree. At the top of the tree, a giant eagle's wings protected the tribes. A Mohawk named Hiawatha traveled from tribe to tribe spreading Dekanawidah's message of peace until the tribes agreed to form the *League of the Iroquois* or the *League of Five Nations*. This wonderful legend made Beautiful Dawn proud to be a Mohawk!

The Mohawk Bowl Game

The Mohawk and other Iroquois enjoyed playing the bowl game with six flat-sided nuts. Sometimes they used clean, dried peach, plum, apricot, or cherry pits ground down smooth and flat on each side. Large crowds gathered to cheer for their favorite person or team. Here's how your class can make and play this authentic game.

What You Need

six flat-sided nuts (such as almonds in the shell) or six buttons for each student
tempera paints and paintbrushes
unbreakable shallow bowl or dish for each group of three to four players

What You Do

1. Have students paint one side of each nut or button black, the other white (or any other two-color combination).

2. Have each child paint the number **1** on each white side and the number **2** on each black side. Let the nuts dry.

3. Divide the class into groups of three to four players. Taking turns, each player puts six nuts into the bowl and shakes it, gently tossing the nuts into the air and catching them again in the bowl.

4. To score, each student adds the numbers that fall face up. For example, if two whites are up and four blacks are up, the score is ten. High score wins the round.

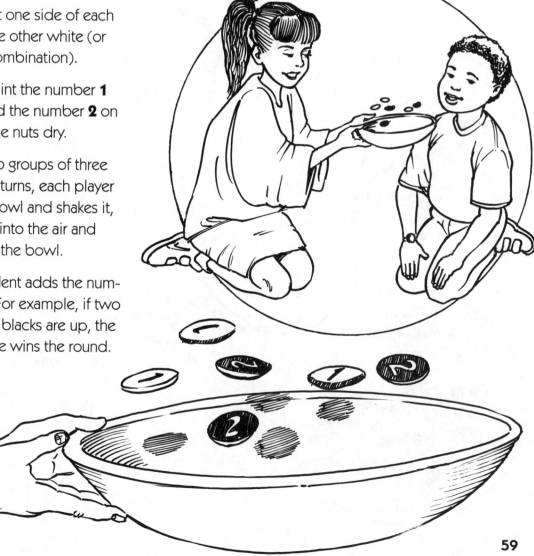

A Holiday Mobile

The Mohawk held seasonal festivals each year. Each festival had its own songs, dances, and prayers.

Color the pictures and cut out the circles. Punch holes at the top and bottom of each circle as indicated. String one long piece of yarn or ribbon through the holes to connect all six circles. Now you have a mobile to hang.

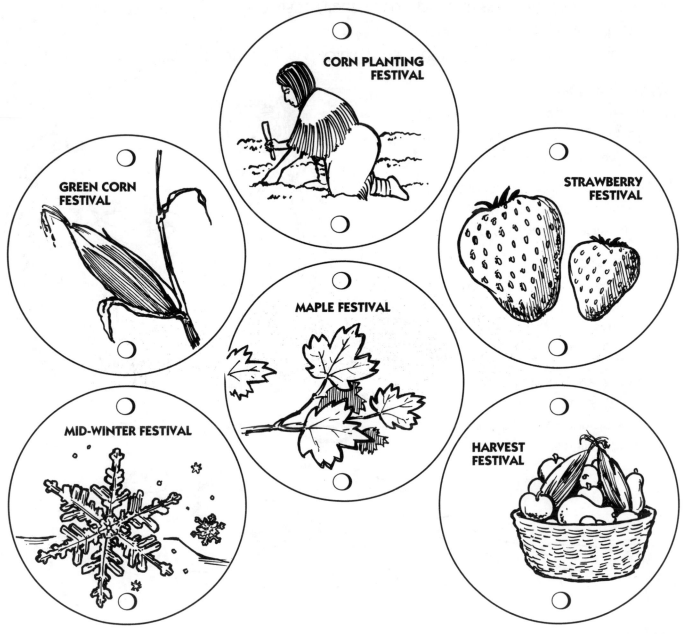

CORN PLANTING FESTIVAL

GREEN CORN FESTIVAL

STRAWBERRY FESTIVAL

MAPLE FESTIVAL

MID-WINTER FESTIVAL

HARVEST FESTIVAL

Name_____ Date _____

Frightening False Faces

When Mohawk people got sick they sent for members of the False Face Society to come and help them get well. The False Face Society wore scary masks carved from tree trunks.

Draw your own scary False Face in the blank space. Color both faces.

Name _____ Date _____

Beautiful Dreamer

A legend tells that the five Iroquois tribes made a peace agreement after a holy man named Dekanawidah had a dream. In his dream he saw the five tribes sitting together under a tree while a gigantic eagle sat on top of the tree with its wings outstretched, protecting the tribes.

In the space below, draw something that you have seen in your imagination or dreams.

MEET THE NEZ PERCÉ

The Nez Percé (*nay per SAY* or *nez purse*) lived in the high plateaus of what is now western Idaho, eastern Oregon, and Washington. The Nez Percé did not need to grow their own crops. They lived off the land all year round. Their rivers were filled with salmon and other fish. Deer, elk, moose, and bear roamed the tall mountains. Broad valleys offered berries, nuts, and the *camas* plant, a root plant.

In the early seventeenth century French fur traders saw some Native Americans wearing bits of shell between their nostrils and named them Nez Percé, meaning "pierced nose." Although called by that name ever since, the Nez Percé stopped the custom of piercing noses by the 1800s.

MAT-COVERED LONG HOUSE

Small groups of thirty to forty Nez Percé would build villages near a river. Several families shared one long, narrow A-shaped house, framed with wood and covered with bulrush mats. Floors were dug at least two feet below the ground. An opening in the center of the roof let out fire-pit smoke and let in light.

The Nez Percé spent almost all their time gathering food. The women and children picked wild berries and other fruits, gathered nuts and seeds, and dug up wild onions, carrots, and roots. If not eaten immediately, these foods were dried or cooked, then stored for the winter.

NEZ PERCÉ WOMAN

From May through November, men and boys caught salmon and other fish. They used traps, nets, spears, hooks and lines, and even bows and arrows. Large quantities of salmon were dried or smoked and stored for the winter. The men also hunted, but because animals were hard to catch, meat was scarce.

Nez Percé first wore clothes made out of tree bark. In summer both men and women wore small, bark-cloth aprons and sandals. Women also wore caps made from dried plant leaves that looked like upside-down baskets. In winter, everyone wrapped themselves in fur blankets. Children dressed like adults.

Life changed for the Nez Percé in the mid-1700s when horses were introduced to them. They became excellent at riding and raising horses, especially the famous *Appaloosa* with its polka dots. They began hunting buffalo and building tipis. They started making buckskin clothing, complete with fringe and beads. Some started wearing feathered war bonnets and became more warlike.

APPALOOSA HORSE

With the opening of the California and Oregon trails in the mid-1800s, settlers streamed into Nez Percé land by the thousands. Some Nez Percé remained peaceful, while others fought this invasion. One of the most famous rebellions was led by Chief Joseph in 1877. When he and his followers were defeated, they were sent to the hot plains of Oklahoma. Many Nez Percé died while waiting for permission to return to their beloved plateau homeland.

CHIEF JOSEPH

64

A DAY IN THE LIFE OF A
NEZ PERCÉ CHILD

White Eagle, the son of a Nez Percé hunter, lived with his family in a small village on the banks of the Wallowa River. White Eagle loved horses and couldn't imagine a life without these beautiful animals. But White Eagle's grandfather remembered what times were like before horses arrived. In the old days the Nez Percé were not buffalo hunters or horse traders. They were mainly fishermen and hunters. Now Grandfather saw his sons and grandsons racing around on horseback, traveling to the Plains to trade, hunting buffalo, and even going to war. All the old men of the village saw these changes. They were not sure that they liked what they saw happening.

White Eagle's father and older brother had left several moons ago to travel in the direction of the rising sun. Over the mountains they would meet with people of the Plains and trade horses for buffalo skins and meat. White Eagle had wanted to go on the trip, too. But Father asked him to stay home and take care of the horses left behind. It was an important job that White Eagle took very seriously.

Father had taught White Eagle all about horses. He knew that the Nez Percé plateau, part forest and part prairie, with mountain streams and rivers, was a perfect place for horse breeding. Horses could stay out on the open range all year with plenty of food available. He also learned that white horses were very valuable. War chiefs liked riding these horses best because they made them feel more important. Also prized were horses with spots on their rumps, which the Nez Percé called *Appaloosa*, after the Palouse River. They were strong, speedy, and gentle animals. White Eagle was proud that his people were famous for their large herds of horses and for being excellent horsemen.

When White Eagle stepped outside his house, it was cold, but there was a hint of spring in the air. Today he would ride out to the valley to check on his father's horses. When he arrived, there were a few other herds grazing together. He was happy that he could pick out every single horse that belonged to his father. He was especially excited to see several foals prancing about on their spindly legs.

On his way home White Eagle passed a stream and was lucky enough to catch two fish. Though they were small, he knew they would be a welcome sight at dinner. All the families were low on stored food. The plants and berries they had dried and put away last fall were almost gone. But with winter over, soon their stomachs would be full again. Tasty camas roots, wild carrots, berries, and delicious salmon would be plentiful in the months to come!

After helping his mother gather firewood, White Eagle sat down by the fire and watched her prepare the evening meal. A pile of smooth stones used to boil the dried camas was heating up in the ashes. Mother cleaned the two fish, cut them into strips, and broiled them over the hot ashes. Next she poured water into a large, tightly woven basket. She added one of the hot stones to make the water bubble and cook the delicious camas. Eating slowly with his horn spoon, White Eagle wished there was more food to go around. But he knew that if he was patient, in just a few moons his father and brother would be home. Then there would be feasting and celebrating for all!

Burden Baskets

Nez Percé women and children spent much of their time gathering roots, nuts, and berries using *burden baskets*. Carried on the back, the baskets had a strap that fit across the forehead. Today's backpacks are a modernized version of burden baskets. Here's how students can make their own.

What You Need

two plain, brown paper grocery
   bags per child

wide masking tape

scissors

stapler

one strip of cloth about one-inch wide
   and two-feet long for each child
   (old pillowcases work well)

paints and paintbrushes, markers, or crayons

What You Do

1. Have each child fit one grocery bag into the other.

2. Cut off the top three inches of paper from the bags.

3. Tape the two bags together around the top edge with wide masking tape. The tape should be half inside and half outside the bags.

4. Let the children decorate the bags with paints, markers, or crayons. They may decorate the cloth strips, too.

5. Staple the cloth strip to the masking tape edge of the basket. This strip must fit across the child's head. Let the children try out their creations by gathering some fairly light items.

Name _____ Date _____

The Four Seasons

Below are the English and Nez Percé words for each season of the year. In each box draw a picture of an activity you do during that season.

WINTER/*ENIM*

SPRING/*ETAIYAM*

SUMMER/*TAIYAM*

FALL/*SAHNIM*

Name_____ Date _____

Chief Joseph

Chief Joseph was a great Nez Percé leader. He battled to lead his people to freedom. But in the end he had to give up. Chief Joseph said, "From where the sun now stands I will fight no more forever."

Here is a picture of Chief Joseph for you to color.

Name _____ Date _____

Horsing Around

The Nez Percé used horses to travel, race, trade, and hunt.

Imagine that you are a Nez Percé chief. Finish the story about the kind of horse you would like to own. On the back, draw a picture of yourself sitting on the horse.

If I were a chief, I'd want to ride on a big _____
(name of color)

horse. I would name my horse _____ .
(name for a horse)

_____ **would run as fast as a**
(horse's name)

_____ . **To keep my horse happy I**
(name of thing)

would feed him plenty of _____ .
(name of food)

MEET THE
SIOUX

The Sioux nation was made up of seven tribes known as the Seven Council Fires. Each Council Fire had its own leaders and camped together. After leaving the Great Lakes area in the late 1600s, the seven tribes moved west and lived in what is now North Dakota, South Dakota, and parts of Minnesota, Montana, Wyoming, Nebraska, and Iowa.

Because the Sioux got almost everything they needed from the buffalo, they followed the herds from place to place. The portable tipi (*ti* means "dwelling," and *pi* means "used for") was the perfect type of home for these wanderers. Made of buffalo hides and wooden poles, a tipi took just minutes to set up or take down. The poles from the tipi were used to make a sled called a *travois* (truh VOY). Before the Sioux owned horses, they used dogs to pull the heavy travois from camp to camp.

Horses, or "spirit dogs," made it easier for the Sioux to move camps. Bigger and stronger than dogs, horses were able to carry larger burdens and bigger travois. And, they made buffalo hunting easier. A man on horseback could outrun a buffalo! A family with many horses was considered wealthy.

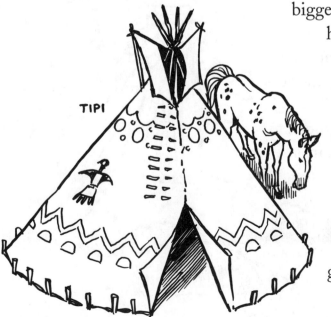

TIPI

Buffalo skins were so heavy, the Sioux preferred deer or elk skins for clothing. Men usually wore only a breechcloth. For cold weather or to dress up, they wore loose shirts and fringed leggings. American cowboys later copied

71

WOMAN'S
DRESS

this style. For special ceremonies men wore headdresses of eagle feathers.

Women wore long dresses with fringe at the hem, sides, and sleeves. They decorated them with porcupine quills, paint, and elk teeth, and later, with glass beads and buttons from white settlers. Moccasins were dyed red, yellow, and blue and decorated with quills. In winter everyone wore buffalo robes. Children dressed like their parents.

Everyone in a Sioux family worked hard. The men hunted buffalo, as well as bear, deer, elk, antelope, wild turkeys, and hens. They made weapons and were the warriors, scouts, and medicine men.

Sioux women were in charge of building, packing, and moving the tipis. They did all the cooking and gathered food such as wild beans, corn, turnips, and berries. Collecting wood and buffalo chips for the fire was women's work. They looked after the children and made the family's clothing from animal skins. Children learned many skills by helping their parents with all the work.

Trouble began as white settlers moved onto Sioux land to farm, ranch, and mine for gold. When the United States Army attacked, the Sioux fought back to protect their families and their way of life. The final fight between the Sioux and the United States Army was at Wounded Knee, South Dakota, in 1890. When this famous battle ended, those Sioux not yet relocated were placed on reservations.

WAR BONNET

BUFFALO

A DAY IN THE LIFE OF A
SIOUX CHILD

Soft Snow lived on the Plains in a land covered by tall grass. Almost everything the Sioux, her people, needed for living on the Plains came from the buffalo. They used every part of the animal—nothing was wasted! Soft Snow's family traveled in a large group that followed the buffalo herds from place to place. They did not grow crops because they were never in one place long enough to harvest them. They did not make pottery because it would break with all the moving.

Soft Snow lived in one big tipi with her parents and two brothers. Her soft, thick, buffalo-robe bed was so comfortable that she couldn't even feel the hard ground beneath her. Sometimes at night she could see the stars through the two flaps at the top of the tipi. When it rained or snowed, the flaps were closed. The tipi stayed warm in the winter and cool in the summer.

Whenever they moved to a new place, the family took along their tipi. Several women working together could set up or take down a tipi in minutes. Each camp was always set up in a shape sacred to the Sioux: the circle. They believed that the circle was an unbroken line to keep good in and evil out. Soft Snow helped to decorate the inside of the tipi. She and her mother painted designs on the walls but never pictures of people or animals. Only the men did that kind of artwork. Soft Snow's father and other Sioux men decorated the outside of their tipis with pictures about their adventures as warriors or hunters, or about a powerful dream. People knew by the designs to whom a tipi belonged.

Soft Snow helped to straighten up inside the tipi. The family stored most of its household goods in several large, strong buffalo-hide containers called *parfleches*. Parfleches were always packed and tied, ready for moving. Sometimes Soft Snow would paint designs on the parfleches in colors like green, red, blue, and yellow.

The morning sun felt unusually warm, and Soft Snow was glad that winter was coming to an end. The winter snows made hunting very difficult. It was hard to see a snow-covered buffalo on the snow-covered Plains. Luckily they had enough food to eat, but Soft Snow was tired of dried buffalo meat. And although she enjoyed sledding on buffalo ribs and sliding and spinning tops on the ice, she was looking forward to horseback riding, swimming, and playing ball. As soon as their scouts sighted buffalo, Soft Snow knew they would be moving camp and that spring would soon follow.

When the scouts finally returned with the news that a buffalo herd was sighted, her entire village was packed and ready to move in about fifteen minutes. Everything they owned could be carried by a person, dog, or horse. The scouts rode out in front with the chiefs and the hunters. The women and children walked or rode behind. No one strayed from the group.

Soft Snow was happy that the hunters would soon bring buffalo. She and her mother would be busy preparing meat, tanning hides, and making new clothes. She looked at the new village, with fires burning inside the tipis like huge glowing lanterns. As the day came to an end, she turned toward the sky and offered a prayer of thanks to the Great Spirit for being so generous to the Dakota people.

Sioux War Bonnet

The Sioux created impressive war bonnets from headbands decorated with feathers. Each feather on a warrior's headdress stood for a brave deed. Some headdresses had long feather tails that hung down in back. Usually the very elaborate ones were worn only on ceremonial occasions. Here's how to help students make their own headdresses.

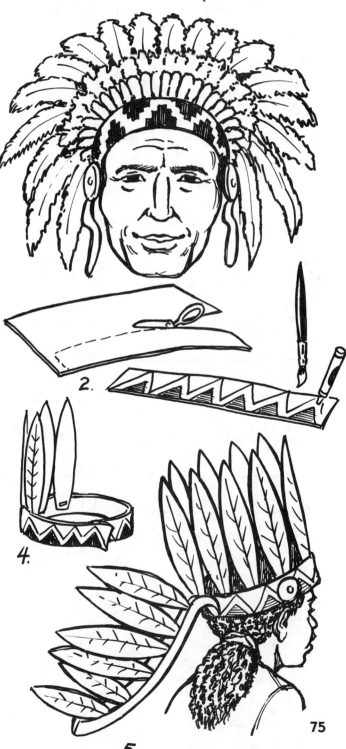

What You Need

construction paper, oaktag, or some
    kind of stiff fabric for the headband
tape measure
scissors
stapler, glue, or tape
seventeen to twenty real or construction
    paper feathers per child, each eight to
    ten inches long
crayons or markers

What You Do

1. With a tape measure, measure around each child's head just above the ears. Add two inches for the overlap fastening.

2. Cut a two-inch wide strip of paper, oaktag, or fabric to the length measured above. If you use construction paper, double for added strength. Give each child the headband to decorate with a design using crayons or markers.

3. Fit the band around each child's head. Staple, tape, or glue the ends together.

4. Staple or glue the bases of the real or paper feathers, side by side, along the inside of the entire headband.

5. To make a single, feathered tail that hangs down the back, have each child attach feathers to a twelve-inch by two-inch strip of paper or fabric. Attach the strip to the headband at the back.

75

Name _____ Date _____

Buffalo ABCs

The Sioux thought that the buffalo was a special gift from the Great Spirit. Almost everything that they needed came from buffalo.

Below is a list of things that the Sioux got from the buffalo. See how quickly you can put the items in alphabetical order.

TIPIS	**CUPS**	**GLUE**	**ROPE**
FOOD	**POTS**	**PAINTBRUSHES**	**DRUMS**
CLOTHES	**WEAPONS**	**SOAP**	**MOCCASINS**
TOYS	**TOOLS**	**JEWELRY**	
SPOONS	**THREAD**	**SHIELDS**	

1. Clothes
2. _____
3. _____
4. _____
5. Glue
6. _____
7. _____
8. Paintbrushes
9. _____
10. _____
11. _____
12. Soap
13. _____
14. _____
15. _____
16. Tools
17. _____
18. Weapons

Name_____ Date _____

Sioux Foods

Here is a list of some Sioux words for foods.

Write what you would choose for breakfast, lunch, and dinner. Use the Sioux words.

Ta-Tan-Ka means *buffalo meat.*

Wa-Ga-Me-Za means *corn.*

Tah-Ca means *deer meat.*

Wa-Sa-Na Papa means *dessert.*

Wo-Ja-Pi means *stew.*

Wa-Ga-Moo means *pumpkin, squash, cucumber.*

Wa-Ha-Pi means *soup.*

Ta-Nee-Ga means *sausage.*

Teem-Chay-La means *turnips.*

~Breakfast~

~Lunch~

~Dinner~

Name _____ Date _____

Tipi Art

The pictures on the outside of Sioux tipis often told stories about a warrior's adventures. Other pictures were of dreams.

Draw your own picture story on the blank tipi below. Use the pictures on this page, or make up your own.

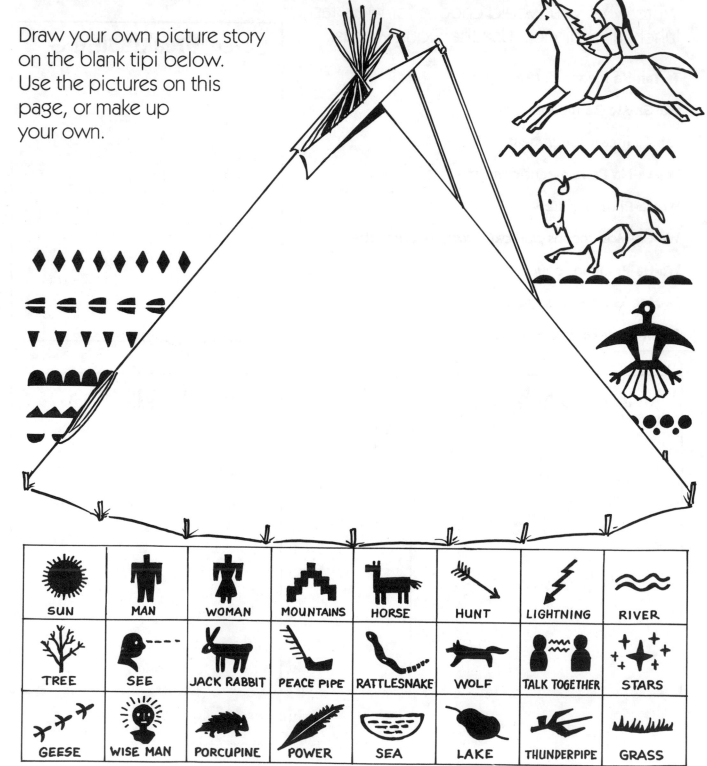

SUN	MAN	WOMAN	MOUNTAINS	HORSE	HUNT	LIGHTNING	RIVER
TREE	SEE	JACK RABBIT	PEACE PIPE	RATTLESNAKE	WOLF	TALK TOGETHER	STARS
GEESE	WISE MAN	PORCUPINE	POWER	SEA	LAKE	THUNDERPIPE	GRASS

MEET THE
TLINGIT

The Tlingit (TLING-git) lived along the coast of what is now southern Alaska and northern British Columbia. They had plenty of food from the Pacific Ocean and the rivers. The forests gave them lots of materials for their houses, clothing, household goods, and crafts. So they were one of the wealthiest Native American tribes north of Mexico.

CEDAR PLANK HOUSE

A Tlingit village was made up of very large, rectangular, wooden houses without windows. These houses were built close together in one or more rows along sandy beaches. The doorways of the houses always faced the water. Some families had a wooden totem pole at the entrance to their house. The carved figures on the pole told a story about the family.

It took a lot of time and many people to build a Tlingit house. Tlingit houses were all built for multifamily use by members of the same clans.

There was plenty of food to go around in a Tlingit family and no need to plant crops. From the ocean the Tlingit caught salmon and seals. Along the beaches they dug clams. They hunted deer, bear, and mountain goats. Women and children gathered seaweed, wild berries, and plant roots.

An important Tlingit food was oil from a small fish called a candlefish.

FISHING

Even when dried out, the fish was so oily that they could put a wick through it and burn it like a candle! They boiled candlefish until the oil came out. Then they separated the oil from the water and stored it in wooden boxes. The Tlingit dipped almost everything they ate into this oil.

The Tlingit needed clothing more to protect them from rain than from cold. In summer most men and boys wore nothing. Women and girls wore only a skirt made of shredded cedar bark. A wide-brimmed basketry hat and a cape of tightly woven cedar-bark matting were worn in rainy weather. In winter they sometimes wrapped themselves in skin or fur robes or in blankets woven from cedar bark and mountain-goat wool. But even on the coldest days, everyone went barefoot.

BLANKET

The Tlingit loved jewelry and wore necklaces, bracelets, anklets, and headbands. They pierced their noses, ears, and sometimes their lower lips. They decorated themselves and nearly everything they owned.

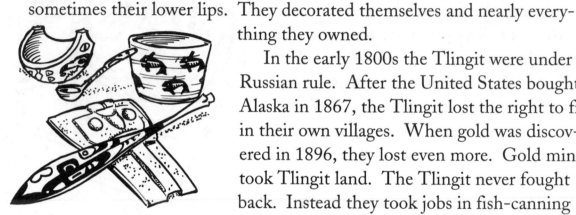

In the early 1800s the Tlingit were under Russian rule. After the United States bought Alaska in 1867, the Tlingit lost the right to fish in their own villages. When gold was discovered in 1896, they lost even more. Gold miners took Tlingit land. The Tlingit never fought back. Instead they took jobs in fish-canning factories in order to survive. In 1971 the United States government gave the Tlingit back some of their land and a cash settlement.

A DAY IN THE LIFE OF A
TLINGIT CHILD

Gray Wolf lived in a beautiful land where his front yard was the ocean and his backyard the forest. His people, the Tlingit, were wonderful artists and craftspeople. It was easy for his family to find food, so they had plenty of spare time to make and decorate things.

Many of the men were skilled woodcarvers, and the women wove special baskets and blankets. Gray Wolf's large wooden house was painted and carved inside and out. In fact, almost everything his family owned was decorated. There were designs of strange-looking birds and animals on canoes, canoe paddles, mats, baskets, blankets, houses, wooden storage boxes, burial boxes, masks, and headdresses. Even fishhooks, paintbrushes, ladles, spoons, and dishes were decorated! By copying his parents, Gray Wolf would learn these crafts.

The Tlingit judged wealth by how many possessions a family owned: food, furs, mats, blankets, carved boxes, jewelry, and coppers (large painted and engraved shield-shaped metal plates). Gray Wolf realized at a young age that the rich men got to own houses and be village chiefs.

In spite of the fog and dampness, Gray Wolf was happy that winter was here. For months his people had hunted, fished, dried, and preserved food. Now it was time for the winter ceremonies, with their songs, dances, and feasts. None of the children wanted to miss any of the excitement.

Today Gray Wolf and his family were going to a great feast called a *pot-latch* (POT lach). One of the richest men in the village had invited others from his own village and from distant villages to the potlatch. Everyone had been talking about it for months. At last the day had arrived!

Gray Wolf quickly climbed into his father's canoe. He was anxious to get to the feast on time. Everyone knew that to be late was an insult to the person giving the potlatch.

The host and his relatives had spent years preparing for this feast. Large amounts of food had been stored up because the feast would last for days, and there would be so many guests. Most important of all were the gifts that the host would give away, such as blankets, masks, carved figures, rattles, carved dishes, wooden or bone spoons, storage boxes, baskets, dried fish or meat, oil, furs, shells, canoes, and paddles. At the feast the host gave away almost everything he owned to prove his wealth and power. The more he gave away, the more honor and respect he gained. He might even destroy some things, just to show how rich he was!

The gift-giving feast was a wonderful experience and Gray Wolf enjoyed the good food, dancing, stories, and, of course, the gifts. He knew that the host would get back as much, and maybe even more, than he gave away. The host of today's feast would be invited to other potlatches in the future and receive many fine gifts. Most Tlingit would try to give the host more presents than he had given to them. So, although a man gave away most of his wealth, eventually he would get back even more!

Totem Poles

The Tlingit were one of the Northwest Coast tribes known for their woodcarving, particularly their totem poles. Totems were not worshipped but were used to illustrate myths or relate a particular family's history. Carved from cedar logs, the totems usually stood in front of houses. Here's how students can make their own small totem poles.

What You Need

one totem pole pattern
  (printed below) for each child
one cardboard tube (four and one-half
  inches long, one and one-half inches
  in diameter) per child
scissors
glue or tape
crayons or markers

What You Do

1. Cut the patterns along the dotted lines and distribute.

2. Have children color the pictures.

3. Have each child glue or tape the colored pattern around their cardboard tube.

Name _____ Date _____

Chilkat Blankets

The Chilkat division of the Tlingit made beautiful and colorful blankets.
The fancy designs were white, yellow, black, and greenish-blue.

Color in the Chilkat blanket pictured below.

Name_____ Date _____

Party Time

At Tlingit potlatch parties the host gave presents to all the guests.
Think of three things that you could give to guests at your potlatch.
Draw the presents on the boxes below. Fill in the names of the people
you would give the gifts to and your name on the gift tags.

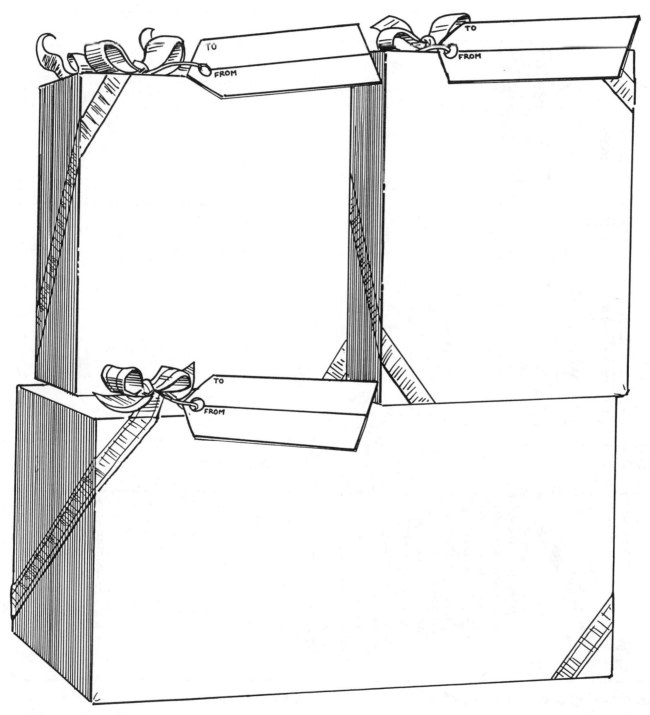

Name_____ Date _____

My Favorite Things

The boxes on the left show some of the Tlingit's favorite things. Draw your own favorite things in the boxes on the right.

Tlingit Favorites   ## My Favorites

Giant cedar tree

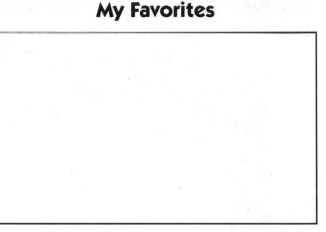

My favorite tree

Salmon

My favorite food

Woodcarving and basket weaving

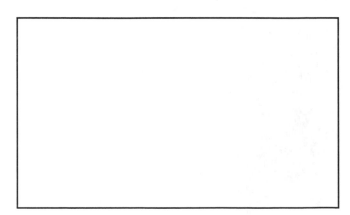

My favorite hobby

SUPPLEMENTARY ACTIVITIES

In this section, you'll find follow-up activities to help reinforce what your students have learned about Native American cultures. These easy-to-do, creative activity sheets are designed for individual and class participation. Children will review some of the information they've already learned and will discover new and interesting ideas.

Name _____   Date _____

House Hunt

It's a double match-up game! Draw a line from the name of the tribe in the first column to the picture of that tribe's home in the middle column. Then draw a line from the picture to the correct name for this type of home.

APACHE

CHEYENNE AND SIOUX

CHIPPEWA

HOPI

INUIT

MOHAWK

TLINGIT

WIGWAM

TIPI

CEDAR PLANK HOUSE

PUEBLO

SNOWHOUSE

WICKIUP

LONG HOUSE

© 1994 by Troll Associates.

See map on page vi for answers to puzzle on page 88.

House Hunt

It's a double match-up game! Draw a line from the name of the tribe in the first column to the picture of that tribe's home in the middle column. Then draw a line from the picture to the correct name for this type of home.

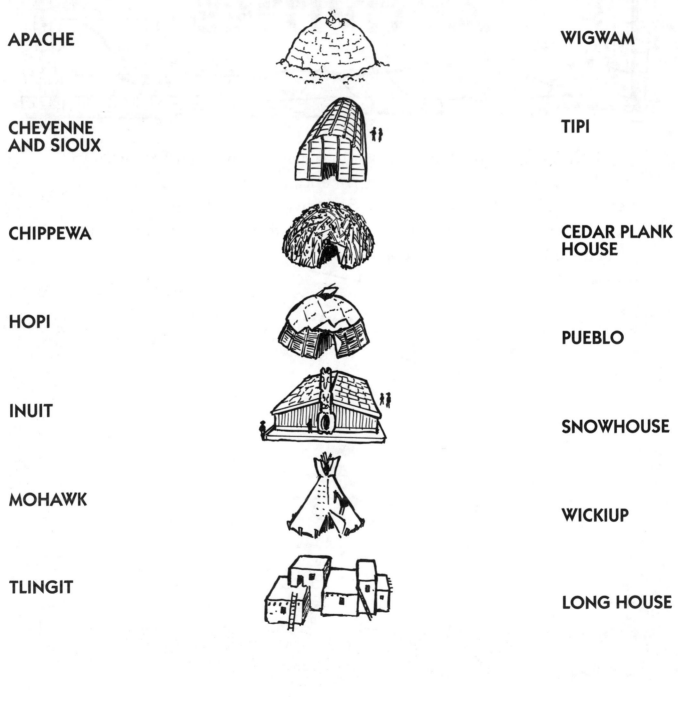

APACHE

CHEYENNE
AND SIOUX

CHIPPEWA

HOPI

INUIT

MOHAWK

TLINGIT

WIGWAM

TIPI

CEDAR PLANK
HOUSE

PUEBLO

SNOWHOUSE

WICKIUP

LONG HOUSE

Food for Thought

The Sioux and the Cheyenne needed the buffalo to survive. The Tlingit needed fish. The Hopi needed corn. The Apache needed the yucca plant. Draw a picture of one food you need. Compare your choice with that of your classmates.

Face Paint

Many Native Americans painted their faces. Sometimes they wanted to scare evil spirits or enemies. Other times they wanted to please spirits or to ask for their help.

Here is what the main colors usually meant:

BLACK = DEATH

RED = WAR

BLUE = SADNESS

WHITE = PEACE

YELLOW = JOY

Color the face on this page. Think about what the colors mean.

Name That State

Fill in the missing letters to find out which state names come from Native American words. If you get stuck, check the list at the bottom of the page.

1. ALA__A__A
2. ARI__ON__
3. AR__A__SAS
4. CON__EC__ICU__
5. I__AH__
6. IL__I__OIS
7. I__W__
8. KA__SA__
9. KEN__UC__Y

10. MASS__CHU__ETT__
11. M__CHI__AN
12. MIN__ES__TA
13. MIS__ISS__PP__
14. MI__SOU__I
15. NE__RA__K__
16. N__W __EX__C__
17. NORTH DA__OT__

18. O__I__
19. OK__A__OM__
20. SOUTH DA__OT__
21. TEN__ES__E__
22. T__XA__
23. U__A__
24. WI__CO__SI__
25. WY__MIN__

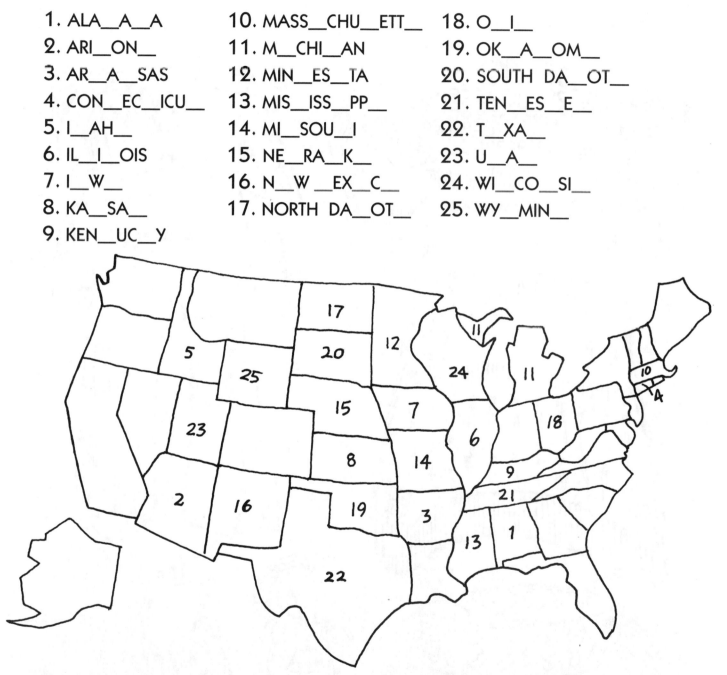

ALABAMA, ARIZONA, ARKANSAS, CONNECTICUT, IDAHO, ILLINOIS, IOWA, KANSAS, KENTUCKY, MASSACHUSETTS, MICHIGAN, MINNESOTA, MISSISSIPPI, MISSOURI, NEBRASKA, NEW MEXICO, NORTH DAKOTA, OHIO, OKLAHOMA, SOUTH DAKOTA, TENNESSEE, TEXAS, UTAH, WISCONSIN, WYOMING

Name _____ Date _____

Dressing Up (1)

Sioux women decorated their clothes for special occasions. They used shells, elk and buffalo teeth, leather fringes, beads, and porcupine quills.

Color these beautiful clothes.

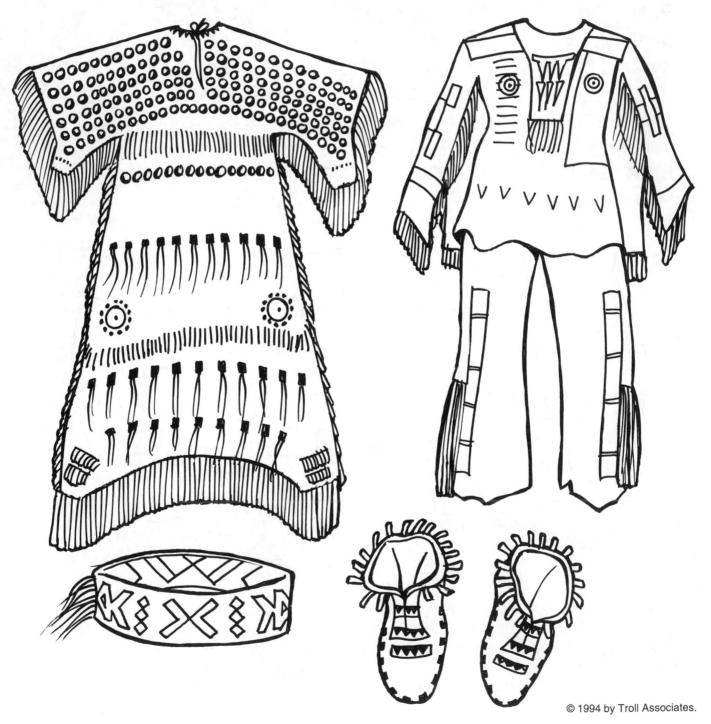

Dressing Up (2)

Design your own decorations for these Sioux clothes.

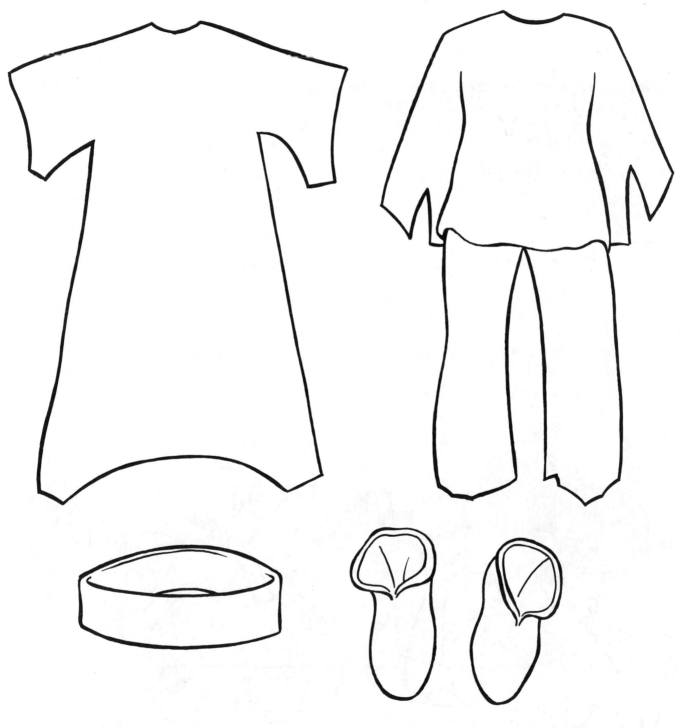

Name _____ Date _____

I Would If I Could

Think about the different Native American tribes that you have learned about. Then fill in the blanks. Share your answers with your classmates.

1. If I could, I would travel back in time to visit the _____ people.

2. I would like to live in a _____ .

3. I would like to taste _____ .

4. I would like to wear _____ .

5. I think it would be fun to _____ .

Native American Match-Up Game

Two people can play this game. (You'll need two copies of each page.) Color all the pictures, then cut out the boxes on the lines.

Lay all the cards face down on a table. The first player turns over two cards. If they match, the player keeps them and gets another turn. If not, the player puts them back where they were. The second player does the same thing. Play continues until all the cards have been picked up. The player with the most matching cards wins.

SALMON

CEDAR TREES

EAGLE

BEAR

HORSE

SEAL

DEER

CORN STALKS

NUTS AND BERRIES

BUFFALO

MAPLE SAP

ELK

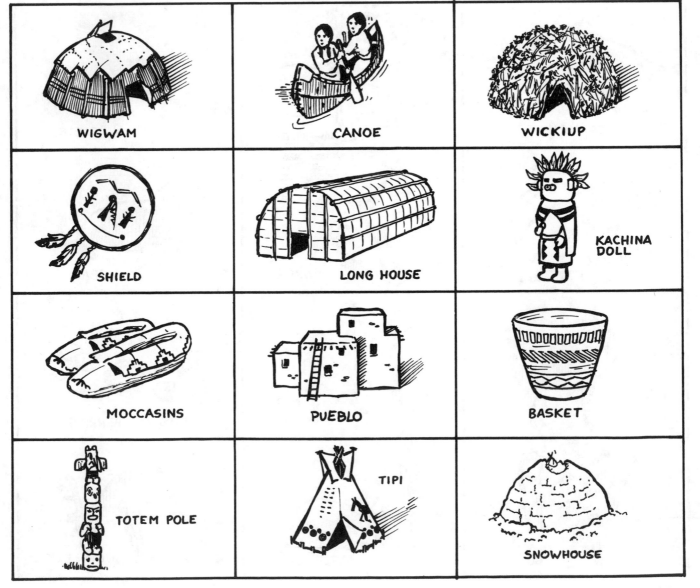

WIGWAM

CANOE

WICKIUP

SHIELD

LONG HOUSE

KACHINA DOLL

MOCCASINS

PUEBLO

BASKET

TOTEM POLE

TIPI

SNOWHOUSE